Getting into

Art & Design Courses

Getting Into guides

Other titles in this series

Getting Into Business, Economics & Management Courses, 9th edition
Getting Into Dental School, 6th edition
Getting Into Law, 8th edition
Getting Into Medical School, 15th edition
Getting Into Oxford & Cambridge 2011 Entry, 13th edition
Getting Into Physiotherapy Courses, 4th edition
Getting Into Psychology Courses, 8th edition
Getting Into US & Canadian Universities, 2nd edition
Getting Into Veterinary School, 7th edition
How to Complete Your UCAS Application 2011 Entry, 22nd edition

Getting into

Art & Design Courses

James Burnett

7th edition

trotman t

Getting into Art & Design Courses

This 7th edition published in 2010 by Trotman Publishing, an imprint of Crimson Publishing Limited, Westminster House, Kew Road, Richmond, Surrey TW9 2ND

Author: James Burnett

4th, 5th and 6th editions by James Burnett
3rd edition by James Burnett and Jonathan Hollins
1st and 2nd editions by Jonathan Hollins

British Library Cataloguing in Publication Data
A catalogue record for this book is available from the British Library

ISBN 978-1-84455-239-9

Typeset by IDSUK (DataConnection) Ltd
Printed and bound by in the UK by Ashford Colour Press Ltd,

Contents

	About the author	**ix**
	Acknowledgements	**xi**
	Introduction	**1**
	What is this book about?	2
	Routes for art and design students	2
	Who is this book for?	2
1|	**Foundation courses**	**5**
	Why do you need to do a Foundation course?	5
	What can you expect from a Foundation course?	5
	Choosing a course	10
	Making the final selection	13
	Checklist	14
2|	**Degree courses**	**15**
	Where are you now?	15
	What is a degree course?	15
	What can you expect from a degree course?	17
	Foundation degrees	22
	Finding the right course	22
	Checklist	26
3|	**How to apply**	**27**
	Foundation courses	27
	Degree and HND courses	28
	The personal statement	29
	Scottish art schools and colleges	33
	Non-standard applications	33
	Preparation for your application	34

4|	**International students**	**35**
	Application deadlines	35
	Interviews	36
	Alternative routes	36
	Fees	39
	English language requirements	39
5|	**Putting together a portfolio**	**41**
	What is a portfolio for?	41
	What is a portfolio?	41
	Which portfolio should you buy?	42
	Getting your work together	42
	Freak-outs	47
	Foundation course portfolios	48
	Specialist course portfolios	51
	Checklist	56
6|	**The interview**	**57**
	What is the purpose of the interview?	57
	What to expect	58
	Preparing	58
	The interview itself: some tips	61
	Checklist	65
7|	**Architecture**	**67**
	Qualifying as an architect	67
	Preparation for your applications	69
	Alternative architecture courses	70
	The personal statement	71
8|	**Offers**	**75**
	Foundation courses	75
	Degree courses	75
	What to do if you do not get an offer	77
9|	**Fees and funding**	**79**
	Foundation courses	79
	Degree and HND courses	79
	Postgraduate courses	79
	Other sources of funding	80
	International students	80
10|	**Postgraduate courses**	**81**
	Types of course	81
	Applying for a postgraduate course	82

11| Careers in art and design **85**

What do art and design graduates do? 87
Where might your degree lead? 88

12| Further information **91**

Applications 91
Funding 91
International students 92
Careers 92
Magazines 92
Websites 92
Art and design bodies 93

Appendix **95**

Institution contact details 95
Non-UCAS institutions 104

About the author

James Burnett is Director of Studies and a careers and university adviser at Mander Portman Woodward (MPW). He has written a number of the Getting Into guides including *Getting into Business, Economics & Management Courses* and he is a regular contributor to the education pages of the national newspapers and specialist careers publications.

Acknowledgements

This book would not have been possible without the involvement of a great many people. In particular, I would like to thank Jonathan Hollins, who was the main contributor to and driving force behind the first edition of this book, and Beryl Dixon for her work on the second edition and the earlier incarnation of the book. Thank you also to Colin Kerrigan, Robert Green and Christine Knau from the University of the Arts International Office, Bill Watson from Camberwell College of Arts, Andrew Watson from Central St Martins, Dr Mary O'Neill and Michelle Palmer from the University of Lincoln, Stella Sinclair from Edinburgh College of Art, Ellie Ducker from the Arts Institute at Bournemouth, David Girling and Sarah Horton at Norwich School of Art, and Caroline Russell at UCAS for their expertise, help, advice and written contributions. My colleagues in MPW's art department (Mark Cheeseman, Louise De La Hey, Kate Brett, Lisa Marklew, Kevin Newark, Alan Shaw, and Julie Standeven) provided invaluable advice on preparing students for their art school applications. Thank you also to Ralph Kiggell, Akiko Hirai and Gerard Hastings for their contributions on the rewards and demands of working as an artist, to Jenny Park, Thuy Nguyen, Evelyn Lu, Ding (Rainbow) Ni, Lei and Lexie, and to the other students who contributed.

James Burnett
February 2010

Introduction

The first decade of the new millennium saw artists rival rock bands, footballers and soap stars in the amount of column inches in the press they received. Headlines advertised the enormous sums of money that were paid for works such as Damien Hirst's diamond-encrusted skull, and large-scale works of art such as Olufur Eliasson's giant sun and Doris Salcedo's crack in the floor, both shown at London's Tate Modern gallery, brought contemporary art to new audiences. Antony Gormley's use of the so-called 'fourth plinth' in Trafalgar Square as a stage for members of the public, or Spencer Tunick's invitation to the public to take off their clothes to be photographed as part of a large crowd, allowed people who had never thought of themselves as part of a contemporary art scene to become involved. Art fairs such as Frieze made art accessible to people who had never been to art galleries, as did the *Guardian's* artist-designed wrapping paper, given away free with the newspaper. People queued to see shows by Gormley, Richard Long and hitherto unknown contemporary Chinese photographers, and the Beijing Olympics 'Bird's Nest' and 'Water Cube' introduced us to a new and exciting world of architecture. The Turner Prize brought arguments and debates that had previously been confined to the art world to a wider public in a way that had not been seen since the Tate's famous 'pile of bricks' controversy 25 years earlier.

The recent recession did not appear to have damaged the art world's interest in artists like Hirst, but lower down the fame ladder there was a definite downturn in sales of art by less well-known practitioners.

But art and design is not just about world-famous painters and sculptors: Tracey Emin's *My Bed*, for example attracted enormous interest. Whatever the merits of Emin's piece, without the skills and abilities of practitioners from a wide variety of disciplines within the field of art and design, it would not have existed and you would not be reading about it now. Throughout its life, from conception to production, exhibition and review, *My Bed* has been touched by artists and designers. Emin, who studied fine art, came up with the idea and oversaw its realisation, furniture designers designed the bed, textile designers were responsible for the linen, an architect designed the building in which the piece was exhibited, a communications specialist designed the catalogue, and art historians and critics reflected on its successes and failures, to name but a few of those involved. A career in art and design could lead you to contribute through any one of these disciplines – or through many others.

In applying to art school you are taking the first step towards what will hopefully become not only your chosen career but also a lifetime journey of experimentation, invention and discovery. Perhaps you already have a strong feeling for a particular discipline, such as fine art, film or fashion and textiles. Or maybe you are unsure which discipline is for you but just know that your instinct to work with colour, line, form, shape and pattern – to question, experiment and explore – is something that you have to develop. Either way, this book is specifically designed for you.

What is this book about?

- Which course(s) should you take?
- Where should you apply to study?
- What should you include in your portfolio?
- How do you prepare for an interview?

This book offers practical answers to these questions and many others, and aims to guide you successfully through the application process.

Routes for art and design students

Entry to an art and design degree is usually a little more complicated than entry to other degree courses – that is one of the reasons that this book has been written. Figure 1 gives an overview of the range of entry routes available; each of these will be examined in detail as the book progresses

Who is this book for?

This book covers the procedure for applications for both Foundation studies and undergraduate degree courses in art and design, and for students thinking about architecture. If you are currently studying at A level you will find all chapters of this guide relevant. However, if you are studying for Applied A levels, a BTEC National Diploma or similar qualifications, you may be tempted not to read Chapter 1. However, it is recommended that you do read it, because it will help you to know what other students have been up to. The entry routes for architecture courses are outlined in Chapter 7.

If you are a student applying from outside the UK or a mature student you will have to think about some other considerations. Most

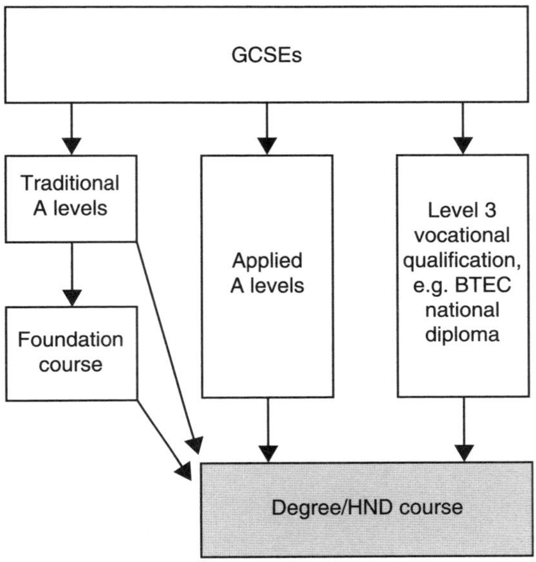

Figure 1 Entry routes for studying art and design

of what is contained in this book will apply, and there is additional information in Chapter 4 and the 'Non-standard applications' section in Chapter 3. Throughout the book, the entrance procedures have been illustrated with reference to A levels. The information is equally relevant to students studying for Scottish Highers, the International Baccalaureate or the Irish Leaving Certificate. If you have any questions about whether your academic qualifications will satisfy the art schools, you should contact them directly.

Read it. No, really! Just having the book on the shelf will not get you into college. Discuss the information and ideas contained within it. Speak to your tutors, friends and parents. You will find it helpful to talk things through. Certain chapters have checklists: use these to help you keep track of your progress. Above all, take action – and when you have finished the book you should have a clear idea of where action is needed. If, for example, you realise that you probably need to do some more life drawing, then go and do some. Admissions tutors are, in any case, always interested in the work applicants have done in their own time, i.e. not just pieces they have done for A level coursework or exams.

You will feel far more confident about your application if you know that you have done everything that you possibly can to help yourself, and reading this book – then acting on what you find out – is the best way to start.

01 Foundation courses

Art and design Foundation courses – the full name is Level 3 Diploma in Foundation Studies (Art and Design) – provide a bridge between the kind of study undertaken at GCSE and A level and the type of work you will do on courses offered at degree level. Although there are exceptions, for those of you currently studying general A levels and hoping to get into art school, taking up a place on a Foundation course will be your next step. Most typically, they are self-contained one-year courses available at a variety of different types of institutions, including universities, art schools and colleges of further and higher education.

Why do you need to do a Foundation course?

If you have not completed an Applied A level or a BTEC National Diploma in Art and Design, a Foundation course will give you an opportunity to find out much more about your creative interests and abilities. You will have the chance to experiment with methods and materials which may not have been previously available to you. You will have the freedom to explore your own ideas and will be truly working for yourself.

What can you expect from a Foundation course?

You can expect to have a lot of fun. While each course will have its own individual style and content may vary, all Foundation courses will attempt to challenge and develop your critical awareness and creative skills. They will help you to select a specialist area of study, prepare your portfolio and make applications for degree courses. There is probably no better way to prepare for a specialist degree course than by completing Foundation studies. Take a look at the views of two students.

> *'For me, an interesting thing about the Foundation course at CSM is that I learnt as much from my fellow students as from the teachers – and this is what we were encouraged to do – they stress the importance of getting inspiration and ideas from peers as well as teachers. In group critiques we listen to everyone*

commenting on other people's work: it is great to see how different the responses can be from different people – this makes the process of talking about art like an adventure as you always find new things and get fresh points of view. There is also a need to teach yourself technical things, as the course concentrates on creativity, so if you need to use unfamiliar software to, for example, make a video, then you have to learn how to do it yourself.'

Evelyn Lu
Foundation course student
Central St Martins

'When I first thought about studying art at university I was pretty sure that I wanted to go down the fine art route, and I was slightly disappointed that I needed to do a Foundation course because to be honest it sounded like a bit of a waste of time. At A level I did some 3D work, photography and textiles as part of the course and the Foundation course just seemed like an extension of this, another year to get through before I could actually concentrate on painting. However, once I had been to some open days I changed my mind completely because I was able to talk to current Foundation students who had felt the same as me but now were loving the chance to experiment with many different media and techniques. As a result of the Foundation course, many of them had changed direction because they had discovered where their true talents and interests lay.'

Peta Edwards

Colleges vary in the ways in which they organise their courses, but in nearly all cases you will choose from the following areas of study:

- **art:** painting, sculpture and drawing; possibly also film and photography
- **communication:** graphic design, illustration and time-based media
- **design:** ceramics, metals, fashion and product design.

Course content is standardised to a certain extent, in accordance with the regulations of the three awarding bodies that validate courses in England, Wales and Northern Ireland. These are ABC Awards, Edexcel and the Welsh Joint Education Committee (WJEC). Under their regulations, Foundation courses are divided into three phases, each phase being roughly equivalent to one of the three terms that make up the academic year.

1| The exploratory phase will give you a general introduction to the theory and practice of art and design. You will have the chance to experiment with a wide range of materials you may not have had the opportunity to use before – including plaster, wood, metal and ceramics, for example – and will work on projects designed to help you to identify your strengths and interests.

2| In the second or pathway phase you will investigate a specialist area of art and design practice, guided by a tutor experienced in that field. At this stage of the course you will also begin to put together a portfolio for degree-course applications.

3| Last comes the confirmatory phase during which you will complete your portfolio, work on a major project (usually negotiated with your specialist tutor) and put together an end-of-year show. The build-up to the end-of-year show and the show itself are things that you won't forget. The Foundation course exhibition might, for example, include static exhibits, multimedia displays and a fashion show.

During the confirmatory stage you will be expected to produce a personal confirmatory study. The following extract from the ABC guidelines gives an indication of what this may involve.

> *Candidates must include in their portfolio of artwork evidence that they can:*
>
> - *research and negotiate a project brief which enables their skills to be clearly demonstrated*
> - *plan and manage their own project effectively to produce a finished piece of work*
> - *create, develop and realise a final outcome within the time available*
> - *select, organise, prepare and display their personal confirmatory study in a professional manner*
> - *evaluate their working methods and outcomes, identifying opportunities for additional development and improvement.*
>
> *Assessment evidence will typically consist of:*
>
> - *records of negotiating and managing the project in an appropriate format, e.g. sketchbook, notes, personal reflective diary, records from tutorials and critiques*
> - a *significant body of work, e.g. research showing a range of ideas, developmental work, final outcomes*
> - *supporting statement, e.g. written and illustrated, audio/video recording.*

Although the three stages are followed by all colleges, tutors have some discretion over the way in which students are taught. There are two main methods. Some colleges during the exploratory phase allocate periods of time to different art and design disciplines, perhaps one week spent on drawing, followed by another on graphics, fine art, fashion, photography and so on. Others prefer to set projects lasting several weeks, which require students to work in several disciplines at the same time.

Students often fall into the trap of assuming that Foundation courses are totally practical. They are not. At least half a day a week will be spent on contextual studies, including the history of art and design, and you will be expected to produce written assignments, including the creation of a personal statement (known as a statement of intent) that outlines, in no more than 500 words, your final major project. (WJEC students produce a 'personal review' instead of a statement of intent.)

Another common mistake is to think that studying on a Foundation course will be rather like being at school, with free periods during the day. Foundation course students work hard! Most courses will run from Monday to Friday, often from 9.30 a.m. to 4.30 p.m. or later. You can also expect to attend at least one evening class a week. Your working week will be divided into studio practice, lectures and seminars, visits and personal study time.

Although there are exceptions, Foundation courses are often very big, sometimes with as many as 400 students all following the same programme of study. For people used to small class sizes, this prospect can be daunting. In practice, nearly all students find that they quickly adjust to their new working environment. Many students find that they really feed off the hustle and bustle that comes with working in large groups and, in part, the course will be about learning to work with others.

Here are some other characteristics of a Foundation course.

- Do not expect lecturers to spend too much time chasing you up. Making the most of the course will be your responsibility. It will be up to you to attend.
- You will find yourself involved in group projects and can expect to forge strong friendships with your fellow students.
- The course will be exhausting at times but it will also be very exciting.

The views of two students and a course tutor given below should give you more of an idea of what to expect and how to make a success of it.

> *'The Foundation course I am on differs from my A level for two reasons. The first is that all of the exercises and projects that we*

do are designed to let us bring in our own ideas and to experiment with things without feeling that every single entry into a journal is going to affect the final marks. The second is how motivated you have to be. At A level, my class was very small and my teacher used to chase me if I hadn't completed something on time. He was always looking over my shoulder, encouraging (and sometimes nagging) me. Here, I have to be more in control of my own work and my deadlines. Although this was a bit difficult at first because I got very involved in all the other things on offer at this place, I now realise that it is an important part of the preparation for my BA course, which will hopefully be in interior design at Chelsea.'

Max Summers
Foundation course student

'I had already achieved the grades that I needed for my business studies degree course, but my aim was to follow a career in marketing, and I wanted to develop my creative abilities prior to starting the course. I decided to apply for art Foundation courses for my gap year, a decision I am really happy with. Rather than spend the year in rather pointless travelling, as some of my friends from school did, I learnt so much about expressing myself creatively, and at the same time making new friends and being able to immerse myself totally in art for nine months. The downside was that I was a bit jealous of the others on my course who were applying for their degree courses at art school, but on the other hand, I was far less stressed than they were throughout the course because I wasn't having to worry about my portfolio.'

Emma
Foundation course student

'The Foundation course combines studio practice, group tutorials, lectures, museum visits, individual and group teaching. It is fast-moving. The students who gain most from a Foundation course are those with the most curiosity. They are the first in the studio in the morning and the last to leave. They participate in all the areas that the course has to offer. They are self-motivated, questioning and do not allow themselves to be defined by the opinions of others. Their personalities will differ widely. They may be extrovert or introvert or all stages in between. They should recognise that a Foundation course is a journey of discovery and that the journey is guided by acts of looking, and they should also know that talent is not enough.'

Bill Watson
International Coordinator
Camberwell College of Arts

Choosing a course

Getting started

Even though Foundation courses now have a national framework, this may be interpreted very differently and what suits one student will not be right for another. You can do an initial search on the internet. Have a look at the websites listed in the Appendix – the great thing about art schools' and colleges' websites is that they are extremely creative and entertaining. You can spend many happy hours investigating them. They are updated and changed on a regular basis and, at the time of writing, particularly good examples include the University of the Arts London (www.arts.ac.uk), Edinburgh College of Art (www.eca.ac.uk), Norwich School of Art and Design (www.nsad.ac.uk), Falmouth (www.falmouth.ac.uk), Glasgow School of Art (www.gsa.ac.uk), the Architectural Association School of Architecture (www.aaschool.ac.uk) and Winchester School of Art (www.wsa.soton.ac.uk).

Next get hold of as many prospectuses as you can and read them carefully. Do not just look at the pictures, but read about the course structure. If you love photography and this does not seem to feature at a college you are considering, you ought to think twice about applying there.

Course content

Look very carefully at exactly what you will be able to study. Consider the course content: is it well structured? Is it flexible enough to allow for personal input? What about the range of subjects covered – is there a wide variety? Although Foundation courses are designed to allow you to gain experience across a whole range of disciplines, they do differ from college to college, and so it is important for you to choose a course that suits your needs. If your aim is to study fashion design at degree level, for example, then you will need to spend at least some of your time specialising in this area of study, so make sure that it is properly catered for.

Location

You can apply anywhere in the country for your Foundation course. However, the majority of students choose somewhere close to home, mostly for practical reasons. These include issues such as accommodation and living expenses, and the reassurance of knowing other people who are at (or have been at) the college. Accommodation, food, travel and materials can be very expensive, and this is a particular issue of concern because a Foundation course is classified as further rather than higher education and you will not be eligible for a student loan. However, UK/EU students under 19 years old are not charged tuition fees in further education. (For further information on funding, see Chapter 9.) This is worth remembering, considering the amount you will have to pay for your subsequent course.

It is also worth bearing in mind that Foundation courses are very demanding in terms of time and energy. It is often hard to combine a Foundation course with a part-time job. However, many students do choose to move away from their local area, either because the local college (if there is one) does not suit their preferences or because they are excited about moving to a new environment.

'Year Zero' courses

In Scotland, the usual system is for degree courses in art and design to be four years in length, with the first year being a diagnostic course – the equivalent of a Foundation course. Several institutions elsewhere in the UK are now also offering this pattern. If you like the idea of continuity – not moving to a different university or college after Year 1 – you might like to look at these options. There are important funding implications though. Year Zero students are enrolled on higher education programmes – which makes them liable for tuition fees. You can find further information on funding in Chapter 9.

Facilities

Questions you may wish to consider include the following.

- How big are the studios?
- Is the light good?
- What are the IT facilities like?
- Does the college have a well-equipped workshop in which you might experiment with a wide variety of materials?
- Is there a photographic darkroom and studio?
- Will you have access to a ceramics studio?
- What is the library like?
- Is there a wide range of books?
- Does it have a good multimedia section?
- Will you have to pay studio fees, and if so what will they be? (See page 24 for further information on studio fees.)

You should also think about other issues: what are the communal facilities (such as refectories, bars and social areas) like? Some colleges are attached to universities and so you might be able to use their facilities as well. However, this might also mean that the social facilities are not on site and so some travelling may be necessary.

You will be able to answer some of these questions once you have read the prospectus or looked at the website, but many questions can only be answered by making a visit.

Open days, visits and speaker evenings

It is vital to attend open days or, if this is not possible because the dates clash with other commitments, to arrange a private visit. The facilities and atmosphere of an art college are the key to whether you will be able to flourish there. Whatever the website says, you will only know whether a particular place is right for you by visiting it. Try to talk to current or ex-students to see what they think of the place. Look at the work that has been produced. Does it excite you? Have a good look at the studios. Check out the facilities – are they really as good as they sound? See if the students are working: a successful studio is one in which people are working effectively – is that the case?

Many schools and sixth-form colleges organise speaker evenings and other special events in which lecturers, course directors and admissions tutors from local art schools, ex-students and other specialists are invited to talk about what to expect when you study art at institutions of further and higher education. Your local colleges may also offer a talk as part of their open day. Make sure that you go! Information straight from the horse's mouth can be extremely useful: you get the opportunity to evaluate not only what is being said but also who is saying it and how. Most visiting speakers will try to give you a flavour of the kind of work that you can expect to be involved with. Speakers are usually happy to answer your questions, they may show you slides or a PowerPoint display to give you an overview of what is on offer. These seminars are extremely useful and are not to be missed.

Atmosphere

Visiting the college is so important because it is the only way to get a feel for its atmosphere. Most people who enjoy art find that the particular qualities of the physical environment and the ambience of the workspace are vital to their creative processes. This varies from person to person, so you will not find league tables ranking colleges in the order of the inspirational effect that they have on their students. Some people like a buzz around them – lots of noise, activity and excitement; others prefer a quieter, more contemplative environment.

How will you know which colleges are right for you? The only way is visiting them and talking to students who are studying there. Never choose a college solely because someone else, such as a teacher or a parent, says that it would be right for you. Trust your own instincts about whether or not the atmosphere feels right. You are the one who will have to work there!

Making the final selection

Using the categories above will have helped you to narrow your choice down to a handful of institutions. It is sometimes helpful to rank your shortlist in terms of location, facilities, the course, atmosphere, etc. You could give the top college in each category five points, the second four points, and so on. Once you have added up the scores, hopefully some clear winners will emerge. The important thing at this stage is to be honest with yourself about how the colleges match up to your requirements. If they do not fulfil your needs, then even if going there 'feels' great it will not be. Make sure that you stick to the criteria and try to establish a clear winner based on the facts. You may well find that a couple of colleges are equally suitable and, at that point, gut feeling may help you to make your decision, but as a general guide stick to facts and not fiction. In other words, do not believe the hype.

Working with your teachers

The final decision on where to go will be yours, but from time to time we can all benefit from a little guidance. Make sure that you work with your teachers. Talk to them. Ask them what they think your options might be. While no teacher is infallible, they will be able to help. Your teachers will probably have first-hand experience of local Foundation courses and will have some information about application deadlines and portfolio requirements. They will know which of the local courses are the most competitive – and whether you would be in with a chance. (Luckily, since there is no limit to the number of Foundation course applications you may make, you can still have a shot at the most difficult to enter while making one or more other applications for safety.)

It is highly likely that your art teacher will be more closely involved with your application than any other person who teaches you, so make sure that you maintain a good relationship with them and try to take full advantage of their expertise.

TOP TIP!

Try to be organised in your preparation. You will need to create a file or folder to store all the forms and information you will receive. Make sure that you keep your diary or personal organiser up to date. If you do not use one, now is the time to start. The last thing you want to do is miss out on the chance to visit a college because you forgot the date of the open day. Do not try to keep all of this information in your head – you will not be able to remember everything. Before making your choice, make sure that you also read Chapter 5, 'Putting together a portfolio'.

Checklist

- ☐ Send off for prospectuses
- ☐ Check out prospectuses, university guides, etc.
- ☐ Check out websites
- ☐ Confirm dates for open days, visits and speaker evenings – and attend them
- ☐ Draw up shortlists
- ☐ Talk things through
- ☐ Make a decision
- ☐ Make your application

02 Degree courses

This chapter provides an overview of degree courses in art and design. It aims to give you a feel for what to expect at degree level and discusses aspects of how to find the right course for you. Architecture courses are dealt with in Chapter 7.

Where are you now?

By the time Foundation students begin the second term of their course, most, though not all, have a fairly good idea of the direction in which their work is heading. Having completed the exploratory phase of the course, in which you experimented with a variety of materials and methods across a broad range of disciplines, you will have chosen a specialist area of study such as fashion, textiles, painting, illustration or product design. By this point you will have begun the process of putting together a portfolio. Alternatively, you may be an Applied A level or diploma student in your second year of study.

In both cases, you will have begun to specialise in a particular area of art and design practice and will be considering your options at degree level. In some cases, although rarely, you will be in the A2 phase of your A levels and considering making a direct application to degree courses.

What is a degree course?

An honours degree course is a specialist programme of study offering students the chance to develop practical skills in, and experience and understanding of, a specific area of art and design. Courses offered at degree level will combine practice with theory and, as such, most will require you to undertake some form of contextual studies alongside your practical work. This will vary from institution to institution and may consist of a formally presented illustrated dissertation or some type of multimedia presentation. All courses will show you how to operate within your chosen area of study at a highly sophisticated level.

Honours degree courses usually last for three years. Most of them are self-validating. (This means that the institutions offering them have the power to award their own degrees.) In some cases, however, such as in smaller institutions, the degree is awarded by a university which validates the course on behalf of the college. Do not worry if an institution does not award its own degrees! Some highly respected art schools which have international reputations and recruit students from all over the world do not do so.

Applications to most degree courses are made through the UCAS system. Although there are exceptions, within the field of art and design there are three broad areas of study available at degree level: **fine art**, **visual communications and design** and the **applied arts**. It is from these three disciplines that you will select a specialist area of study.

Specialisations found within the areas of visual communications and design or the applied arts typically aim to prepare you for the workplace and, in that sense, may be highly vocational in nature. Sometimes they will include a period of work experience. Courses based on fine art, such as painting or sculpture, will be more geared to professional studio practice (although your creative skills may also be valued by industry).

There are essentially four different types of degree you can choose to take: single or combined honours, or a modular or sandwich degree.

Single honours

Most art and design students studying at degree level in the UK follow this type of course. Competition for places at well-known universities and colleges is strong. Courses at colleges with international reputations (and there are many) attract enormous numbers of applications. Places at these institutions are as hard won as for any other type of undergraduate study. Courses typically run for three years and will require you to complete some form of moderated study of the history of art and design. You will have to pass this element of the course in order to be awarded your degree.

Joint honours

These courses make it possible to combine the study of distinct but often complementary subjects, for example, art and psychology at Reading University.

Modular degrees

These courses enable students with a wide range of interests, including those outside the field of art and design, to combine the study of a variety of subjects. At Oxford Brookes University, for example, history of art can be studied in combination with many other subjects (including languages, arts management and English).

Sandwich degrees

These may be any of the above course types, but will also contain some form of structured work experience. Most typically this will take the form of a 'year out' beginning at the end of the second year, in which you will work in industry, returning to complete your studies in the fourth and final year.

A year abroad

Some courses provide an opportunity for students to spend a period of time studying overseas. For example, Leeds University offers four-year International or European Fine Art programmes which include up to a year of overseas study in Europe or North America. For further details, you should look at the college or university websites.

What can you expect from a degree course?

Because you will be studying for three years or more and will be concentrating your efforts in a specific area of art and design, on a degree course you can expect to develop high levels of expertise. Degree courses should offer you excellent facilities and technical support within your chosen area and will also provide you with access to resources outside your specialisation, often by means of reciprocal arrangements with other institutions. You will be asked to consider issues and ideas at their most fundamental level and will be encouraged to fully realise your creative potential. You can expect to enjoy the full range of extracurricular activities that are available to all undergraduates.

> *'My Foundation course was a lot of fun and I knew early on that I wanted to go on to do a degree, although it took a while before I was sure which area to specialise in. In the end I followed my instinct – I have always loved to paint. I knew London fairly well, having stayed with friends a couple of times, and was keen to move away from home.*

'The course has been a real challenge. I didn't expect to be pushed so hard – I really had to think things through and talk to the other students and tutors about my ideas and opinions. I found this very difficult to begin with, but you get used to it eventually – we were all in it together.

'I knew from Foundation that I would have to work hard, but some aspects of the course surprised me. At school I hadn't really thought of myself as particularly academic and was dreading the written project. In fact I turned out to be pretty good at this sort of stuff! The social life was brilliant, although by the end of the second term I was exhausted. You really can't party all night and work all day.

'Taking a degree course was an excellent decision. I am a very different person from the one who started the course. My work has changed too. I intend to continue painting, but I also want to carry on writing as well. I have just written an exhibition review for my local paper.'

Jason Michaels
BA (Hons) Fine Art Painting
Middlesex University

Edinburgh College of Art: extracts from course introductions

The following will give you a more detailed idea of what might be involved in some of the degree specialisations.

BA (Hons) in Painting

This programme guides students towards an individual and appropriate means of expression in the context of contemporary fine art practice. Each student will be able to synthesise and innovate, communicate in a team and work independently, opening up a wide range of career possibilities. The initial stages of the Painting programme offer a broad range of timetabled study and supervision, equipping students with technical skills and enabling them to develop individual and group approaches. From Year 3, each student has an individual studio space and by final year, they work independently with tutorial guidance. While painting is central to the programme, our students have opportunities to explore their ideas through photography, video, printmaking and computer-generated imagery.

BA (Hons) in Sculpture
Our students are given a firm grounding in the conceptual and technical processes involved in the making of contemporary sculpture, and can explore a wide variety of ways to realise their personal ideas. In addition to the studio-based practice, professional practice skills, research, drawing, visual thinking and art theory form the main structure of the programme and all programme elements collectively underpin and inform the making of work. A valuable interface exists between the practice and the theory component, which is delivered by Visual and Cultural Studies staff, and some three-way tutorial discussions between the individual student and staff from Sculpture and Visual and Cultural Studies are an integral part of the programme.

BA (Hons) in Photography
The programme is designed to prepare our students for a career in photography, not only by providing them with knowledge of equipment and technical facilities but also by encouraging each student to develop their personal vision of the world. Even a limited study of the art and science of photography quickly reveals the need for specialised ways of looking and seeing.

The programme adopts an eclectic approach to the medium of photography. A great deal of practical experience is required in order to realise fully the medium's potential. At ECA, technique is regarded as a means to an end rather than an end in itself, and the keeping of notebooks is encouraged to help you maintain and develop a broad visual vocabulary.

Students explore a wide range of fine art and commercial practice, using traditional photographic hardware as well as the latest computer technology. In keeping with this holistic philosophy, still image, moving image, and multimedia production are all possibilities within the programme.

Degree course specialisations

There is an enormously wide variety of specialist courses available at degree level (see Figure 2). Some disciplines will be familiar to you, while others will be entirely new.

The following pages list some of the courses available.

Taking the three general areas of study already mentioned as a starting point, the following lists are designed to give an overview of some of the courses available. These lists are not definitive – new courses are being set up every year. Please note that some specialist areas of study

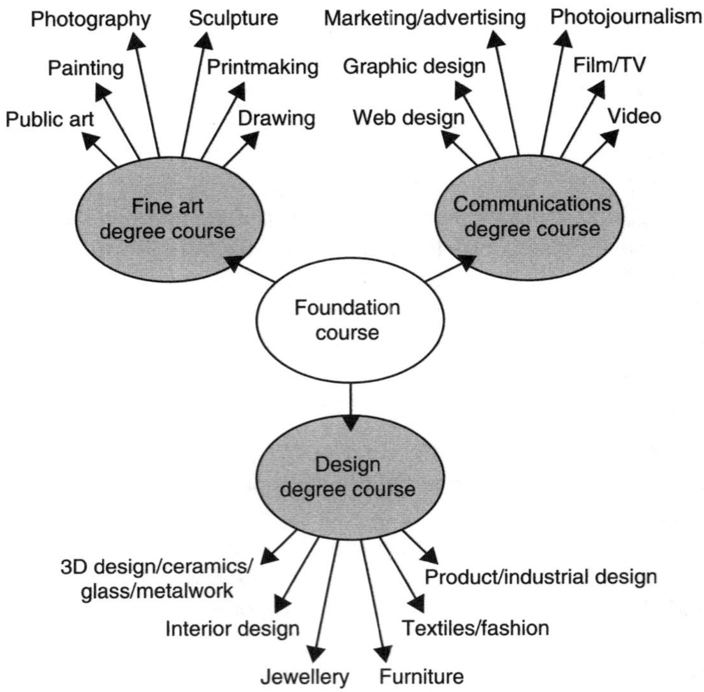

Figure 2 Courses available after completion of a Foundation course

appear in more than one list. This is because a subject such as photography, for example, could be studied in the context of the fine arts, with an emphasis placed on personal self-expression, or might be offered as a visual communications course if it concentrates on preparing you for a career in photojournalism.

Fine art

These courses, which place an emphasis on personal creativity and self-expression, can cover a wide variety of disciplines and often include:

- drawing
- painting
- photography
- printmaking
- sculpture
- tapestry
- textile studies.

Visual communications

These courses are typically vocational and can sometimes include a period of work experience:

- advertising
- advertising and editorial photography
- animation
- biological imaging
- corporate identity
- film and television
- forensic photography
- graphic design
- graphic design and advertising
- illustration
- lettering
- photography
- print and graphic communication
- public art
- typographic design
- visual communication design
- wildlife illustration.

For an example of a graphics show, please see Plate 3 in the colour section.

Design and the applied arts

Again, these courses are usually vocational in nature and often aim to prepare students for professional practice:

- architectural glass
- ceramics
- conservation
- fashion
- fashion design with technology
- furniture
- glass
- interior design
- interior textiles and floor coverings
- jewellery
- knitwear design
- museum and exhibition design
- performance costume
- product design
- silversmithing
- swimwear
- textiles
- theatre: designing for performance
- transport design.

So far, we have been talking about honours degrees, but a new type of degree course is now available – which you might like to consider.

Foundation degrees

Foundation degrees have been available since autumn 2001 and are on offer in a wide range of subjects. The title is a little unfortunate where art and design are concerned – since it could be easily confused with Foundation courses! The new courses are a qualification in their own right and can also lead on to an honours degree course. Designed in consultation with employers, they are courses that train people in specialist career areas and develop:

- work skills relevant to a particular careers area
- key skills, for example, communication and problem solving
- general skills, such as reasoning and professionalism.

If you do a Foundation degree you will be able to choose between entering employment and continuing training in your job, or converting the qualification into an honours degree through further study, usually by transfer into the second or third year of a related degree course. Foundation degrees are available in a range of disciplines including graphics, fashion, interior design, three-dimensional design and digital media design. A full list of courses and more information can be found in the Foundation degree section on the UCAS website (www.ucas.com).

Finding the right course

Most students applying for places on specialist degree courses are either attending, or have been to, art school. Perhaps you have been studying close to home and want to move further afield, or perhaps you are well established where you are. You may have a pretty good idea of what you are looking for, but try to keep an open mind. Do your homework. Get hold of as many prospectuses as you can and read them carefully. Do not just look at the pictures, but read about the course structure and content. If you plan to study furniture design, for example, and love to make things in the workshop, make sure that the courses you are considering are supportive of this approach. Use the internet – the great thing about art schools' and colleges' websites is that they are extremely creative and entertaining.

Course content

How will you know which course is going to suit you? For example, what is the difference between studying a BA in Glass and a BA in Architectural Glass? Degree courses in specific subjects will differ from college to college. Some illustration courses, for instance, will place more emphasis on digital manipulation while others will focus more on traditional drawing techniques – so it is important for you to understand exactly what is being offered. Take full advantage of the literature available. Make sure that you read and fully comprehend the course specification. If you are unclear about anything, try to speak to the course director or head of school. Look very carefully at exactly what will be studied, at what point in the course, for how long and how much flexibility and choice you will have. For example, if you want to become a forensic photographer, make sure that you are not applying to a fine art photography course! Since many art and design graduates work as freelances it is important for them to understand how to run their own businesses – about finding premises to work in, tax and legal requirements, how to calculate costs when pricing their work – and how to market their work and present it to prospective employers or buyers. If you think you may freelance in the future, ask now whether the course contains modules on self-employment, given either by course tutors or by the college or university careers service.

Location

You can apply anywhere in the country for your degree course. Consider the practicalities, such as the cost of accommodation and travel. Moving to a big city may be attractive but will you be able to afford it? Many students enjoy and benefit from the dynamism that city life can offer; some prefer to live and work in a quieter location. What will be right for you? For many students it is essential that they are close to galleries and museums. What are the local facilities like? Do they meet your needs? Higher education is expensive and, although you may get some financial help, nearly all students have to raise funds privately. If you are planning to work part time, are there job opportunities?

> *'Firstly, I would have never thought of changing my career if I had not come to London. Many short courses were available at the time I came to London and therefore it was very easy to start something new. You are also encouraged to study further if you are enthusiastic about the subject. From a practical point of view, there is a great deal of cultural diversity co-existing in London. It helped me clarify my own cultural identity and aesthetics, what I see as beauty as well as learning from other cultures. The Western way of seeing things seemed to conflict with my idea of beauty. However, in the latter stages it helped me develop my own*

visual language and learn how to convince people how and why I see things in my own very specific way.'

Akiko Hirai
Ceramicist

Facilities

Does the college have the facilities that you will need to study your subject? A degree-course studio should be very well equipped. Make sure that the relevant technology is up to date and kept that way. As well as working within your own field you may well need to cross over into other areas of art and design. Many art schools have reciprocal arrangements with other institutions. Do these exist and will they be practical? If, for example, you intend to study sculpture, you will no doubt be looking for spacious, well-lit and well-equipped studios, but what about the IT facilities? Remember that you will have to put together some kind of contextual study. Are the computers up to the job and could you use them to create 'virtual' sculpture?

As your skills develop, so will your needs. Try asking yourself the question, 'Do I know what all the equipment is for?' If you do, then the course probably is not well equipped.

You should also think about communal facilities such as refectories, bars and social areas. Some colleges are attached to universities, and so you might be able to use their facilities as well. However, this might also mean that the social facilities are not on site and so some travelling may be necessary.

Student support

Does the institution provide good welfare arrangements, such as student counsellors and an accommodation office?

Studio fees

Most institutions charge students studio fees. These can vary considerably from place to place and, although they are not likely to influence your final decision when compared with other factors, it is worth finding out what they are and what facilities you get for the money. (This is not something that is usually quoted in prospectuses or course leaflets.) 'Studio fees' is a bit of a misnomer since it sometimes also includes course materials. It is also worth enquiring about prices of materials sold in the university or college shop, if this is the system that applies. You could check also – perhaps by asking a student on a visit day – whether the final degree show involves students in much expenditure. You will be able to answer some of these questions once you have read the prospectus or looked at the website, but many questions can be answered only by making a visit.

Open days and visits

It is only by visiting a course that you will get a feel for its atmosphere. Most artists and designers find that the physical environment and the ambience of the workspace are vital to their creative processes. This varies from person to person, so you will not find league tables ranking colleges in the order of the inspirational effects that they have on their students. But ask yourself 'what is the vibe like?' It might suit other people, but will it suit you? Make a point of talking to students who are studying there. Is the working environment a productive one? Can you picture yourself in it? Never choose a college solely because someone else says that it would be right for you. Trust your own instincts about whether or not the atmosphere feels right. After all, you are the one who is going to study there!

Past students

It is always interesting to look at the names of practising artists who have graduated from the university or art school. Although famous alumni do not necessarily make one institution better than another, they can act as a guide towards the type of work that is being undertaken there. And if an artist you really admire studied on one of the courses you are investigating, this can add to the attraction of the college.

The final choice

Remember that you are going to have to live with this decision for three or four years, so try not to be carried away by a sudden rush of blood to the head. As important as it is to trust your instincts, using the steps outlined above to narrow down your choice to a handful of institutions will help you make a decision you won't regret.

Go through this list and think things over carefully. Talk things through with those people who know you best – you will benefit from a second opinion. Rank your shortlist in terms of location, facilities, the course, atmosphere, etc. Try giving the top course in each category five points, the second four points, and so on. Use the scores to help identify which course meets your requirements. You will probably find that there are two or three courses that are up there. Do not be afraid to trust your instincts, but make sure that your shortlist is based in reality and not fantasy. Read the lecturer's view below on making that final choice.

> *'When prospective students are considering Lincoln I would always suggest that they visit on an open day if possible or make an appointment with the programme leader if they can't make an open day. You cannot decide from a website or a prospectus. I would also suggest that they should meet a current student on their chosen programme. A student will be able to answer those awkward questions that might be difficult to ask at an interview and will also give an honest feel for the place. This is especially true for mature candidates who might be a little unsure about returning to higher education. Mature students are always happy to share their experiences.'*

Dr Mary O'Neill
Senior Lecturer in Cultural Context
Higher Education Academy Teaching Fellow
Faculty of Art Architecture and Design
University of Lincoln

Checklist

- □ Send off for prospectuses
- □ Check out prospectuses, university guides, etc.
- □ Check out websites
- □ Confirm dates for open days, visits and speaker evenings – and attend them
- □ Talk to tutors
- □ Draw up shortlists
- □ Talk things through
- □ Make a decision
- □ Make your application

03 How to apply

This chapter explains the procedures for applying for Foundation, degree and Higher National Diploma (HND) courses. However, before you apply, you need to do lots of preparation. If you have not already done so, you should read the relevant sections on choosing a course in Chapters 1 and 2.

Foundation courses

In most cases you apply directly to the art colleges for entry to their Foundation courses, and you can apply to a number of colleges simultaneously, since there is no central application scheme. However, there are some exceptions to this. For example, if you wish to apply for a place at the University of the Arts London (Camberwell, Central St Martins, Chelsea, London College of Communication, London College of Fashion and Wimbledon) you need to obtain a common application form from one of them, then send it to your first-choice college, naming a second choice as well. (If your application to your first-choice college is unsuccessful, your application form is then passed on to the second choice.)

The application forms vary from college to college. All require basic details about yourself and your education, but they differ in the amount of space (if any) that you have to write about yourself and your interests – the personal statement.

Unlike the UCAS scheme for applications to degree courses (see page 28), there is not one date by which all applications must be submitted. The closing date for applications varies from college to college, and so you must do your research early and make sure that you do not miss any deadlines. The closing date for applications is often the end of January, but this is not true for all colleges, so consult the prospectus or the website well in advance.

Most Foundation course applications need to be accompanied by a reference, usually from the head teacher or head of art at your school or college. If you are a mature student or are not studying art at school, you should read the section on non-standard applicants (page 33). Warn the person you choose to do the reference well in advance that you are going to apply, and ask them whether they are willing to act as a referee. References usually take time to write, so do not surprise your referee with a form the day before the deadline. Even if he or she does manage to write it in time, it is less likely to be full of the necessary detail, and it will certainly not emphasise your planning and organisational skills! Bear in mind that you are applying for a place on a practical course, and so the application form is only the starting point. The key elements of the selection process are the portfolio and/or the interview. Admissions staff will place most emphasis on evidence of high potential and creative ability. See Chapters 5 and 6 for more information. If your initial application is successful, you will be either asked to deliver (or send) your portfolio to the college so that it can be assessed by the selectors, or asked to attend an interview either at the same time as your portfolio is reviewed or later.

Degree and HND courses

If you are applying for honours degree courses, Foundation degree courses or HND courses, you normally do so using the UCAS system.

Almost all applications are made online using the UCAS Apply system. Further details can be found on the UCAS website and in the book *How to Complete Your UCAS Application*, but a brief overview of the process is given here. Up until 2009 entry, to apply for art and design courses you would have used what were called Route A and/or Route B applications. The deadline for Route A courses was 15 January, and students could not express a preference on the UCAS form – the Route A courses were listed alphabetically. Route B courses were chosen sequentially, and the deadline was late in March. For 2010 entry onwards, the system has been simplified.

- Applications for all art and design courses are made on the same UCAS form, at the same time. The sequential element of the old Route B system has gone.
- Institutions indicate whether the application deadlines for their courses are 15 January (equivalent to the old Route A system) or 24 March (as was the case with the Route B system).
- Under the old system, some courses could be chosen as Route A or Route B. This will no longer be possible.

Further details are available on the UCAS website, or from the institutions themselves.

The personal statement

If the colleges that you apply to require a personal statement (remember that applications submitted through UCAS always do) you need to plan this very carefully, as it will significantly affect your chances of gaining an interview or being offered a place.

Some application forms only allow you to write a few lines to support your application, and they generally specify the information that they are looking for. For instance, the form used by Hereford School of Art provides five lines and asks applicants to comment on their interests in art and design, how these have developed and why they believe that the course is suitable for them. Clearly, with so little space, your statement needs to be carefully planned. A good response might include a list of your particular interests, but you must make sure that they match the facilities that the college has to offer.

Many application forms give you enough space to write 200–300 words in support of your application, and the UCAS online application form gives you 4,000 characters.

You should try to cover the following:

1| introduction: reasons for wanting to study art
2| reasons for choice of college
3| interests within art: areas of art that you enjoy, e.g. fine art, graphics
4| influences: artists that inspire you, exhibitions that you have seen
5| a description of some of your own recent work
6| career plans or future areas of specialisation – if known
7| other information: interests, work experience, travel.

A sample personal statement can be found below. It is for a Foundation course and is thus institution specific (the space available is more than you would usually get). A UCAS personal statement would not include those elements, unless you were applying to only one institution.

In the second paragraph, the applicant has mentioned that she went to an open day. Attending open days is important if you are to convince the admissions tutors that you are serious about your application. More information about open days is given on pages 12 and 25.

The best way to demonstrate your enthusiasm for art is to talk about your own work. This also gives the admissions staff an idea of your interests in a specific, rather than general, way. In the fourth paragraph, the applicant has mentioned some of her favourite artists. It is a good idea to try to include a contemporary artist, as you want to show the selectors that your interest in art is a developing one and that you are keen to be part of the current art scene rather than immersing yourself wholly in the past.

Personal statement: example 1 (word count 629)

I enjoyed art at GCSE and decided to continue it at AS and A level. A level gave me the chance to experiment more, and to include ceramics and photography in my work. In my spare time I take evening classes in life drawing and always carry a small sketchbook with me so that I can make notes on things that inspire me. A Foundation course will give me the chance to investigate many new areas, such as graphics and design, and will help me to make the right choice for my degree course.

I would like to study at Melchester School of Art because I was impressed by the facilities, particularly the light and spacious studios. When I came to the open day, I met many current students and saw their work, and I felt inspired by what they had achieved in such a short time. Everyone that I met was very encouraging and enthusiastic, and I felt that I could be extremely motivated if I came to you. I also came to your inspirational graduate show and I hope to be able to follow a degree course here after the Foundation course.

At the moment I am working on a piece on the theme of 'identity' and I am trying to incorporate objects and images that have special significance for me into a large mixed media piece. I got the idea for this project after seeing Masao Yamamoto's installations of photographs at the Hackelbury Gallery near to where I am studying. He ages and distresses his tiny photographs so that they look like part of his history, and then displays them in combinations that make you want to try to guess the (nonexistent) 'story' behind them. I have also become interested in how the perception of objects can change depending on how they are viewed, following a visit to an exhibition of photographs from last year's Jerwood Photography Awards. I was fascinated by Kevin Newark's series 'Protoplasm': his images of discarded plastic bags floating in a canal reminded me both of exploding galaxies and microscopic bacteria because there was no way of referencing the scale of the images.

My favourite artists are Matisse and Antony Gormley. Pieces from my own AS work have been influenced by some of Matisse's later works, particularly his Blue Nudes. I went up to

Gateshead to see Gormley's 'Angel of the North' and then to Liverpool to see his figures in the sea. Recently, I went to see the Rothko exhibition at Tate Modern (in fact, I went back many times) and was excited by his use of black paint – I never knew that there were so many shades of black. I am now working on a series of photos based on this, by overexposing images when I take the photo so they are almost completely white, or in the darkroom so they are almost completely black. The works of Ori Gersht and Paul Graham have also played a part in this project.

I am not sure in which area of art my future lies, but at the moment I am interested in stage design and fabric design, although I have not had a chance to do this at school. However, last summer, I spent a week at our local theatre and was able to help the set designer work on the backdrops for a production of 'The Tempest'.

Apart from visiting galleries and exhibitions, I enjoy music (I play the drums in a band, and have passed Grade 6 on the clarinet) and going to the cinema. This summer I am going to travel through Europe by train with some friends, and hope that this will give me inspiration for future work. My sketchbook will be with me all the way.

Notice, also, that the personal statement includes details of exhibitions that the applicant has visited, and what she found interesting in them. Never drop in the names of artists or galleries/exhibitions that you have visited without giving some indication of why they are important to you. The point of the personal statement is to demonstrate that you not only enjoy art in a practical sense, but you also think about it.

WARNING!

Do not put things into the personal statement simply to impress the selectors. If you do get to the interview stage, you may be asked to talk about one or more of the artists or exhibitions that you have mentioned, and the surest way to be rejected is to be caught out.

Another key element in the personal statement should be something to lead the reader to ask you a specific question at interview for which you have prepared an outstanding answer. In the third paragraph, the applicant describes, briefly, her own work but does not give much detail. She can be reasonably confident that, if she has an interview, she will be asked more about these pieces of work, and so she can prepare for this part of the interview in advance.

What to avoid

The personal statement is just that – a statement that reflects your interests and influences. There are some things to avoid at all costs.

- You must avoid using very general statements that say nothing about you. 'I have always been interested in art, and get great enjoyment from my work', without an explanation or description of specific areas of interest or pieces of work, will not give the selectors anything to go on.
- Writing 'I would like to come to your college because of the facilities' is too general: say which facilities and why they attract you. Bring in your own areas of interest if possible.
- Never make judgements about artists, their work or exhibitions without backing them up: 'I went to see the Howard Hodgkin exhibition at Tate Britain, and I liked it' is not going to impress anyone. The admissions tutors would be more won over, however, if you added 'because it was fascinating to see how he developed his own unique style over several decades. I liked his use of wooden panels instead of canvas, and the fact that he often painted the frames onto the panels. Although his work is very abstract, each of the paintings is very personal, representing people he knows, events or places he has visited. Many of the paintings took several years to complete, with layers of paint being added years after he started them.' Similarly, writing 'we were taken to see Peter Beard's photographs at the Michael Hoppen Gallery – I didn't like them' doesn't provide the reader with any information about you unless you explain why you didn't like the work.

From the Ruskin School of Drawing and Fine Art website:

> *'Ruskin students often remark that the Foundation year represents a vital breathing space in which to focus and research, and to develop new working relationships. When the Ruskin staff look at the portfolios of applicants we are always looking beyond the fulfilment of school curricula. We look for highly motivated activity over and above any project-based work. We look for a breadth of engagement, a sense of purpose and a strength of opinion in the way the portfolio is edited. We*

enjoy discovering a sense of the temperament behind the work and any other interests which inform the portfolio. We are emphatically not looking for a formula or a style but do seek signs of energetic, ambitious and inquisitive work.'

Richard Wentworth
Ruskin Master

Scottish art schools and colleges

As already mentioned in Chapter 1, the system in Scotland is slightly different: most degree courses are four years in length and incorporate the equivalent of a Foundation course. In some cases, students can enter the second year directly if they have undertaken a suitable foundation or portfolio preparation course. For details, you should contact the institutions directly. In both cases, application is made through UCAS.

Non-standard applications

Not everyone who applies for Foundation courses is an A level (or equivalent) student. Similarly, some people apply for degree courses without having studied on a Foundation course. The main categories of 'non-standard' applicants are mature students (for further and higher education purposes, anyone over the age of 21) and overseas students. If you fall into one of these categories, you should make direct contact with the colleges that interest you to discuss your situation.

The colleges' websites and prospectuses will also contain sections aimed at you. It is important to be aware that, for all applicants, in addition to your personal qualities, the portfolio is the most important element in the application. Without a promising portfolio, you will not be offered a place. Make sure that you read Chapter 5, which offers detailed advice on this.

Mature students

You may already have either a portfolio of work that you have done when you were at school (in which case, it will probably need updating), or perhaps a collection of pieces that you have been working on recently. It is often helpful to get guidance from art teachers, and for this reason many mature students will take evening classes, portfolio classes or Access courses before applying.

(Sometimes this is best done at the college to which you intend to apply.)

Application to postgraduate courses is covered in Chapter 10.

Preparation for your application

Make sure you stand out from the others:

- visit galleries and exhibitions on a regular basis
- keep a notebook and a small camera with you at all times to record things that interest you
- try to get your work exhibited in school exhibitions, your local library, local cafes – anywhere where people will see your work.

04 International students

Students from all over the world come to the UK to study on art or design courses. Many UK institutions are recognised internationally as being the best in the world. Last year, over 3,000 overseas students gained places on art or design degree and HND courses. Of these, about half were from countries from outside the EU. Many of these students will have followed Foundation courses in the UK for a year. If you want to be a fashion designer, an architect, a product designer, or if you want to train to work in the creative sides of TV, film, IT or advertising, studying in the UK will give you the best possible preparation and qualifications.

Students who are interested in architecture may already be aware that the regulation of architectural training in the UK means that UK architecture qualifications will allow them to work anywhere in the world. A significant proportion of the most exciting and high-profile architectural projects around the world in recent years have had an input from architects trained in the UK.

Most of the information contained in this book applies to international students as well as to home students. However, some aspects of the application procedures are different and if you are applying to study art or design at Foundation, degree or postgraduate level, you should be aware of these. The main differences are listed below:

- application deadlines
- interviews
- alternative routes
- fees
- English language requirements.

Application deadlines

You should read the information on application routes and deadlines contained elsewhere in this book. If you are applying for a Foundation course, you should also check the individual institutions' websites because deadlines vary from college to college. In some cases, international students from non-EU countries can apply for these courses later than UK or EU students, and the dates for interviews may also be later in the year.

Interviews

In order to be offered a place to study art or design at an art college or a university, someone from that institution will need to look at examples of your work. If you live in London and you are applying to an art college in London, this process is easy: you turn up for an interview carrying your portfolio. During the interview, someone will look at your work and discuss it with you. If you live 8,000 miles away, however, attending an interview is more of a problem. Art colleges and universities approach this in a number of ways:

- you send examples of your work by post
- you scan your work and email it
- you are interviewed in your own country
- you attend an approved course either organised by, or recognised by, the university.

Some institutions, such as the University of the Arts London, run portfolio preparation courses in a number of countries, successful completion of which will result in the offer of a place. Another option is a portfolio review session: the institution will organise events throughout the world where students can bring their work to be looked at and discussed with teachers. Details of these courses and events can be found on the institutions' websites, and are also advertised locally. Under some circumstances (e.g. if you are considered to be too young for direct entry onto a Foundation course, or if your English is not sufficiently good) you may be advised to spend a year on a pre-Foundation course at a recommended school or college in the UK before proceeding on to the Foundation course (see below).

Alternative routes

Most international students will follow the same route as UK students to their degree or postgraduate art and design courses, that is, a Foundation course, followed by a three-year BA course and then, in some cases, an MA course. However, because pre-university art education varies considerably in content and delivery from country to country (for instance, in the balance between technical skills and original ideas), some international students are not accepted directly onto Foundation courses. Others may have the potential to start a Foundation course but they may be too young or have not reached the required standard of English. Students in this situation may be advised by universities or art schools to spend an extra year in the UK prior to the Foundation course.

A popular route is to spend a year in a UK school or college either following an art 'pre-Foundation course' (art and design-related and, if necessary, English courses) or studying on one-year accelerated A level courses. This route would be recommended by the university or art school at the interview or portfolio review stage. Many art schools will have partner institutions that can provide these courses.

An alternative route for those international students who are too young to go directly onto an art Foundation course is to attend the International School of Creative Arts (an independent boarding school near London), which opened in July 2009, in association with the University of the Arts London. The school provides pre-university training for British and overseas students, which will prepare them to enter a university course in the arts and related disciplines. In addition to two-year A level courses in a range of art and design subjects (with the option of adding academic subjects in combination with these), the school also offers a two-year portfolio programme, designed for those who possess the academic qualifications for university entrance but need to develop a portfolio. They also offer a fast-track foundation programme. Further information can be found on the school's website (www.isca.uk.com).

'The majority of our courses at the University of the Arts London are studio/practice-focused and as such entry is generally based on portfolio assessment and interview. Therefore, careful preparation and selection of the portfolio is an essential preliminary to the interview.

'The portfolio is a visual diary. It is the documentation of the individual's journey, both perceptually and conceptually, over a period of time. In essence the portfolio should be comprehensive, demonstrating a breadth and depth of inquiry, curiosity and genuine investigation. Solid practical skills and experience of working with a variety of media and techniques are, in addition, of equal importance.

'The portfolio should include work done in school or college and at home. The range of approaches and the materials used should show that the applicant has made the most of the opportunities around them, both in terms of what they are being taught and the art room or studio facilities that are available. We particularly

look for evidence that an applicant has been prepared to develop some ideas further on their own initiative and in their own time.

'Time and care is needed in selecting the portfolio, and systematic decisions about what to include and how to organise and present the work should be made. Obvious repetition should be avoided, as should over-selection. A limited number of relevant works in progress may be included because, first and foremost, we are looking for potential.

'Ideally, a portfolio should consist of between 25 and 50 pieces of recent work, completed over a two-year period. This collection of work should show evidence of a broad-based creativity and include sketchbooks, visual research books, idea sheets and any experiments or explorations in three dimensions. The portfolio should demonstrate, through project and thematically based work, evidence of individual creativity and the development of ideas. Generally, it is important that work reflects and demonstrates creative thinking and a personal commitment to a particular project.

'In the early stages of all our courses we concentrate on combining technical workshops with set projects. As courses progress, assignments generally become more wide-ranging and contextually based. All practical work is undertaken within a framework of individual and group tutorials as well as studio criticism sessions, where all students are encouraged to offer constructive critical opinions and advice to each other. Critical exchange and dialogue is central to our teaching approach.

'Therefore, at interview all applicants are expected to discuss and evaluate the development and context of their work so as to demonstrate broad understanding and an ability to think critically.

'A portfolio does not supplement an interview, but is the main factor in assessing a student's future potential. Thus the portfolio is even more essential to students who are unable to be interviewed.

'You should present your portfolio in the form of colour photographs, colour photocopies, slides or CD. It is best not to send originals in the post. You should send between 25 and 50 pieces of work. The portfolio should ideally be approximately A4 size if being sent by post.

'University of Arts London have representatives in a number of countries across the world. Our representatives can assist with

all aspects of the application procedure, offer information about programmes and courses and assist with immigration matters.

'When our senior academics make their next scheduled visit, a local representative can arrange for applicants to have an interview or an advice session with an academic. Our contact details and an overseas schedule can be found on our website.'

Robert Green
Manager of International Student Support
University of the Arts London

Fees

The fees for Foundation courses for non-EU students are between £7,000 and £9,500. For degree courses, they are likely to be between £10,000 and £14,000 per year. Living costs could add an extra £9,000–£10,000 a year. Postgraduate courses can sometimes be less expensive than degree courses. Check the institutions' websites for more information. US students may be able to get US Federal or private loans. Further information on fees and funding can be found on the UKCISA website (see full contact details on page 92).

English language requirements

You should refer to the individual institutions for their requirements. To give you an idea of what level of English is required, the University of the Arts London gives this advice:

'The ability to understand, communicate and learn in English is an important requirement for acceptance into University of the Arts London. If English is not your first language or primary language, you must provide us with evidence of your English-language ability (such as an IELTS score and certificate).

'You can apply before you have the required level of English language ability. The requirements for entrance to full-time courses are shown below:

- *Fashion portfolio: IELTS 4.5*
- *Foundation studies, diploma, Access and ABC diploma courses: IELTS 5.0*
- *Foundation degree: IELTS 6.0*
- *Bachelor of Arts, postgraduate certificate and postgraduate diploma: IELTS 6.5*
- *Master of Arts: IELTS 7.0.'*

05 Putting together a portfolio

For most students making the move into further or higher education, the offer of a place is normally made on the basis of past academic performance, personal statements and references, predicted grades for forthcoming examinations and, increasingly, an interview. With art school applicants, all of the above applies but with one very important addition: you will need to show the college your work. Whatever the particular format your interview may take (discussed in Chapter 6), you will turn up with your work, the college will look at it and you will get the chance to talk about it and yourself, as well as to ask and answer questions.

For some this may seem a daunting prospect. Most artists worry about showing their work to others. It is not surprising when you think about it. Having put our heart and soul into what we do, naturally we worry about negative judgements. Do not panic! Attending an interview with a portfolio of your work gives you a big advantage. Unlike your contemporaries who rarely get the chance to show what they can do except in exams, not only do you get to show what you are best at – being creative – but you also have plenty of time to prepare in advance, a good idea of what to expect, and all the people interviewing you will be artists themselves so they will understand what you are doing.

What is a portfolio for?

All of the colleges that you apply to will be interested in your qualifications, references and experience, but above all they will be concerned with who you are, what you have done and what your potential is. Demonstrating these things is the function of the portfolio.

What is a portfolio?

A portfolio is a folder containing examples of art and design work. Professional artists and designers need to take their portfolios to job interviews. You will show your portfolio to the admissions tutors of the courses to which you apply. Portfolios come in all shapes and sizes and in many cases you will be able to use the same one (normally A1 size) in which to display your work for both Foundation and degree applications (though obviously the contents will be different!).

There are some exceptions. For example, a student applying for a specialist degree course in photography might choose to use a portfolio specifically designed for that purpose. They are often smaller and are sometimes referred to as 'books'. In fact, the term portfolio can be used to describe any collection of works for presentation even if they are not actually displayed exclusively in a folder.

Which portfolio should you buy?

At this stage, do not buy one at all. Wait until you have read the whole of this book, have had a chance to think things over and, most importantly, have some idea of what you are going to put in it. As a guide, buy the best one that you can afford, as it will protect your work better and be a saving in the long term. Look at the quality of the zip if it has one and check that the ring binder works well. Is the handle strong and comfortable? When thinking about sizes, consider how big your work is. On the other hand, do not bite off more than you can chew. If you cannot carry it, it is too big! Above all, though, remember that it is the quality of your work that counts and not the quality of the thing that you carry it in.

Getting your work together

The following guidelines apply to portfolios for both Foundation and degree course applications. Read them carefully: they describe the qualities that you should look for in your work and will help you make decisions about which pieces to select. Later in this chapter there are also sections giving guidance on the requirements for each type of portfolio. Make sure you read the contributions made by course tutors.

The first step in putting together your portfolio is to gather together all of your work. When you do this it might be tempting to say, 'I won't need that' or, 'That's no good', but at this stage just concentrate on getting all of your work in one place so you can see what you have got: finished pieces, unfinished pieces, sketchbooks, models, notebooks, written work, old work, new work – get everything! This is important because not only will you find things that have been tucked away that are actually very good, but also as you look through your work you will begin to see relationships emerging between new and old pieces. A small sketch that at first may seem rather unimpressive might have inspired a later, much more accomplished piece. The ability to make judgements and to evaluate what you have done, to recognise a good idea and to develop it further, is an important part of the creative process. Admissions tutors will be assessing to what extent you are able to do these things.

It may help you to organise your work into categories. The following list will provide you with a starting point:

- contextual studies/written work drawings from observation
- drawings of invention
- finished pieces
- life drawings
- models and maquettes
- sketchbook/journals
- sketches and studies
- works in progress.

The importance of drawing

Albert Einstein used the formula $E = mc^2$ to express his famous theory. Scientists use mathematics to express and explore their understanding of the world and how it works. Artists and designers do this with drawing.

Drawing could usefully be described as the act of making marks to convey meaning. Artists and designers use drawing to record observations, work out ideas, pass on information, express feelings and emotions and resolve practical problems. Drawings are often used to help us visualise how things fit together. For example, scale drawing can be used to work out whether all the units of a kitchen will fit into the space available. Diagrams and flowcharts can be used to demonstrate how ideas and principles relate to each other. Drawings come in all shapes and sizes and are made with a variety of different purposes in mind. Examples of types of drawing include:

- life drawings
- observational drawings such as those done from a still life or made in the field (e.g. architectural details)
- plans and designs
- sketches and drafts.

Whichever course you apply to, the admissions tutors will want to see your drawings in one form or another because they are evidence of your visual intelligence. Your drawings demonstrate that you can perceive, understand, invent and communicate visually. These abilities are at the core of successful art making.

Sketchbooks

Sketchbooks fulfil many purposes. They are a place in which artists and designers begin the creative process. They are also a place in which to store cuttings, postcards and virtually any other articles that will fit. They are the place in which you can put your ideas, thoughts and feelings down on paper. Typically, interesting sketchbooks contain visualisations of many types, made by you for a variety of reasons.

These images might take the form of carefully studied observational drawings or quick sketches or doodles. In a sketchbook you will refer back to previous ideas and make relationships between the images on one page and those on another. Perhaps you have spent some time experimenting with different ways of making marks. You will be familiar with many of the effects that you can get with a pencil, but what kind of drawings could you make with a nail? A sketchbook or journal is the place where you might try something like this. Maybe you have been using your sketchbook to work out the volume of a space so you can calculate how much concrete you would need to fill it? Why would you want to know? At this stage you are probably not completely sure and you do not need to be.

The sketchbook is a place where you can try things out even if they seem crazy; it will reveal the extent of your curiosity. In this sense, sketchbooks can be highly personal and frequently become much cherished. They also provide evidence of your creative development because they are time based.

With very few exceptions, all courses will want to see your sketchbook work.

Project work

Project pieces might be two or three dimensional or time based and may use a variety of media. Normally they will have been completed on your current course of study and will show to what extent you have taken advantage of the training and support you have been given.

The ability to undertake and complete a project, whether it is self-determined or in response to a set brief, is one of the qualities that prospective art schools and colleges look for. Work developed over an extended period – formed by experimentation, contemplation, reflection and risk taking – says a great deal about its creator.

- Are you willing to stick with something to the end?
- Will you test a theory to the point of destruction?
- Can you keep an open mind?

A project piece will demonstrate your imagination, invention and skill and give evidence of your willingness to condense your theories and commit to a final outcome. If it has been made as part of a group project it will also show your ability to work with others. It can also be very helpful to include some work in progress in your portfolio. Unfinished pieces can have a freshness and ambiguity that often stimulates conversation.

Overly prepared portfolios in which everything is polished to perfection may come across as stifled and dishonest. Including an unfinished piece or two will help to avoid this problem.

Personal work

Most artists and designers have a strong desire to be creative. Whether they are extrovert or introvert by nature, creative people have a need to express themselves. Inevitably, this does not stop when you leave the classroom or studio. Personal work may take a variety of forms, but its essential qualities are that you did it because you wanted to, it contains your own opinions, thoughts and feelings and was made to fulfil your needs. Maybe you feel strongly about something and want to make a point or perhaps you are in a band, have recorded a demo and need a CD cover. In both cases, you would naturally have a need to create. Personal work says a lot about who you are and demonstrates your passion and commitment.

Contextual studies/written work

Written work is often overlooked at interview but should be included if possible. At degree level it will be a requirement to complete some form of contextual study, and on a Foundation course you can expect to be fully engaged in critical thinking (although you probably will not be required to produce an extended written piece). Reflecting on the work of others and responding to its qualities is a fundamental part of the creative process. This work will give you the chance to demonstrate your ability to explore ideas and concepts, learn from the work of others and, in many cases, will show how you are able to make choices about typefaces, justifying text and formatting illustrations.

Matching your portfolio with the course specification

Make sure that you read the course's portfolio specification thoroughly. Talk things through to make sure that you are clear about what is required. Each course will have its own requirements. For example, many courses ask you to limit your portfolio to a particular number of pieces. Whatever the requirements are, respect them: they will be there for a reason and are your best guide to what to include. In many cases it will be necessary for you to adapt your portfolio for each course to which you apply. Make sure that you give yourself time to do this.

Special considerations

It may not be possible to take all of your work to the interview; perhaps it is too big or too fragile. For practical reasons, art schools and colleges inevitably have to put some restrictions on what can be accepted. If this is the case, in most instances it is perfectly acceptable to take slides or photographs, but do check with the admissions tutor first. Original work is preferable if possible, and if you do take photographs make sure that they are good ones.

Label your portfolio

Make sure that you clearly identify your work. You do not want there to be any confusion about who did it and you want to make sure that you will get it back. This is particularly important if you have to submit your portfolio in advance of the interview – do put your name and address in an obvious place.

Enrolling on evening courses

Evening courses can be a valuable source of extra tuition. They give you a taster of what being at art school is like and can be a lot of fun. For mature applicants, they provide the opportunity to work with teachers and become reacquainted with a teaching environment. If you do not have access to a life model, for example, consider taking life-drawing classes. Courses could be theoretical in nature and could cross over into other disciplines that are new to you, for example animation. Not only will this help to build up your portfolio, but it will also be an excellent demonstration of your commitment.

Portfolio reviews

Many schools and colleges offer portfolio review sessions, sometimes leading up to mock interviews. Certainly your teacher or tutor will offer you advice and support. Remember, you are not always the best judge of what to put in and what to leave out of your portfolio. You are going to need a second opinion, and taking the advice of an experienced teacher will help enormously.

Freak-outs

Most artists feel overwhelmed from time to time – it often goes with the territory for those of us who are willing to test things to the limit. The process of putting together a portfolio can feel stressful at the best of times and if you leave everything to the last minute it will be even worse. You also need to make sure you leave time to think about what you are going to say at interview.

When a group of A level students applying to art school was asked 'If you could give a fellow art school applicant one piece of advice on how to put together a portfolio, what would it be?' their unanimous response – which they all shouted out – was 'Start early!' Setting manageable weekly deadlines and keeping an honest record of what you have and have not done will help enormously. Set specific goals such as 'I need more life drawing'. Not convinced? Read on.

> *'My friend was rejected by her first choice because she was so nervous at the interview that she couldn't talk about her work at all. I probably overcompensated by talking too much at first about all the things I had rehearsed, but the interviewer soon relaxed me and I began to enjoy the conversation. He was able to get me to talk about how I really felt about my work and what I wanted to do with it.'*
>
> **Ellie**

> *'As an A level art student, there were a lot of things I should have done to prepare which I didn't. What I didn't do was consider going to art college early enough. I applied in January but I hadn't really started researching art colleges until the month before. Because of this I was late in starting to put my portfolio together. Fortunately, I had regularly attended life-drawing classes so I had plenty of drawings to choose from, but if I hadn't, there would not have been much time to do anything about it. I have still got a lot to do and my interview is only a couple of weeks away. I really wish I had started earlier.'*
>
> **Jerome**

> *'At the time, I was disappointed not to be going directly to the university. However, the one-year A level courses I took gave me*

a chance to experiment with new techniques and to gain confidence. I got two A grades and this made me feel much more sure of my own abilities when I started my Foundation course.'

Monica

[Monica came from Korea and spent a year in London studying A levels in Art and Photography. She had been interviewed in Korea by the University of the Arts London, which recommended the A level route. Her interviewer was impressed by her portfolio, but felt that it lacked variety. Monica was 16 years old when she was interviewed, and would have been too young to start a Foundation course at the university.]

'There was a lot of variation in the interviews I attended. At one art college, we discussed our work in small groups and so we were able to see what other students had brought along. This was a bit intimidating as some of them had produced amazing things. At another college, I was interviewed on my own, and was able to discuss my work with one of the teachers from the college. Although I was put on the spot a bit more, I preferred this because I felt more at ease talking without an audience!'

Kay

[Kay attended several interviews for Foundation courses.]

'If I had to give prospective students one piece of advice, it would be to practise talking about their work with their teachers before going to the interview. Talking about your own work is difficult even when you know the person you are talking to, and in an interview it is very stressful unless you have practised beforehand. I felt such a phoney when I was talking about why I had created the pieces in my portfolio for the first time, but it got easier the more I did it. My A level teachers at my college helped me by organising mock interviews before the real thing.'

Jenny

Foundation course portfolios

This should contain as wide a variety of work as possible. You may think that you are heading for a career in fashion design, but you are applying for a diagnostic course that aims to confirm that choice for you or point you in another direction. Tutors want to see potential in all sorts of areas, so include:

- colour work made in a variety of media
- contextual studies or written work
- drawings and paintings made from observation and imagination, using a variety of media
- examples of design work and model making
- life drawings
- multimedia work such as video
- photography
- photographs of three-dimensional work if it is not possible to transport it
- printmaking
- project work made on your current course and for yourself
- sketchbooks.

Don't worry if you cannot include all of these; very few students are able to. Remember that admissions tutors will primarily be looking for potential and motivation.

> *'The portfolio tells us about you. It tells us what art and design experience you have had and what kind of course you have followed. It tells us about your imaginative and creative responses to ideas, to observations, to process and to concepts. The portfolio will be looked at to assess the individual candidate's enthusiasm, creativity, intellectual and practical skills in the practice of art and design.*
>
> *'Consideration will be given to the candidate's potential for further development and progress in any of the fields of art and design the College has to offer. The admissions panels will also be looking for signs of the following student attributes:*
>
> - *strong portfolio displaying research, visual and manipulative skills based on the portfolio grading system used in First Year Studies at ECA*
> - *a willingness to broaden the existing skill base and to be fully committed to a broad, general, diagnostic first-year course, leading to specialist study in the second year*
> - *good communication skills – visual, verbal and written*
> - *an inquisitive nature and an ability to demonstrate intellectual curiosity*
> - *self-motivation and drive*
> - *organisational skills (timekeeping, presentation of folio, etc).*
>
> *'The portfolio should include representative examples of work undertaken as part of a programme of study and/or personal research. The compilation of a portfolio should not be regarded as an end in itself, but rather as one of the results of that study. The portfolio is the primary means by which a candidate presents*

her/himself to the admissions panels and it should be prepared accordingly. Logical presentation assists in this and there is much to be gained by grouping work in categories such as drawing, painting, two-dimensional design and so on, in chronological order. It is also valuable to be able to trace the development of a work and preliminary studies are best presented with the final work.

'There should be evidence of study and investigation, the exploration in depth or in breadth of a subject/interest in a sustained way. Portfolios should display, in some form, evidence of developing skills relevant to artistic practice – for example drawing skills, colour investigation, making skills, photographic skills. Alongside these there should be evidence of a lively interest in the collection of relevant research materials such as: photographs, magazine articles, historical data, collected objects and personal notes.'

Birgitta MacDonald
Director of First Year Studies (Art and Design General Course)
Edinburgh College of Art

Guidance on portfolio preparation for Foundation courses

'A portfolio is essentially a well-presented collection of a student's visual work. Portfolios may vary in size, shape and number of works included, but broadly should demonstrate visual skills alongside imagination, invention and a personal approach to ideas and concepts. All the work need not be "finished". Interviewers are interested in the creative process. What was the idea? How was it researched and developed? Were a single or many resolutions possible? The sketchbook or workbook is important in this process. It can reveal visual thinking alongside written notation. In interviewing, many reviewers find a student's potential is evident in the sketches, doodles, scratching, half-formed ideas and cartoons of a sketchbook. A "finished" work may say one thing but a workbook says many.

'If paintings or sculptures are included, how did they come into being? Was their source from the visual world – a museum, gallery or public event? Or was it from the studio – a life drawing or still life? Did it arrive from a memory, photograph, a written text or a piece of music? Can the portfolio show the development and growth of a visual idea?'

Bill Watson
International Coordinator
Camberwell College of Arts

Specialist course portfolios

While this portfolio should contain a range of work demonstrating your all-round ability, you will obviously need to demonstrate a commitment to a particular area of study and show a level of skill and ability in that field. However, admissions tutors will be realistic about the extent to which you will have been able to develop your skills and will be very much looking for potential and motivation. Items to include are:

- colour work made in a variety of media
- contextual studies or written work
- drawings made from observation and imagination, using a variety of media
- life drawings
- personal work in your specialisation made for yourself
- photography
- photographs of three-dimensional work as required, if it is not possible to transport it
- project work in your specialised area of study made on your current course
- sketchbooks.

With respect to your specialist project work, use the following examples as a starting point for ideas on what to include. As a rule, your portfolio should contain a sustained project made within your proposed area of study. Contact the course admissions tutor if you are unsure what to put in.

Fashion

Drawings; sketches; fashion designs; photographs or actual examples of garments you have made; a collection of information on particular designers, fashion manufacturers or shops; a design project worked on to a brief; evidence that you read fashion magazines and follow developments on the catwalk.

Film, TV and animation

A short film that you may have made as part of a course project; scripts; storyboards; a subject-dedicated sketchbook; evidence that you regularly watch films and read reviews.

Fine art

Paintings and/or sculptures, photographs, textiles and pieces of work, produced to a negotiated brief; original pieces, produced entirely from your own ideas; evidence that you read art magazines and visit exhibitions.

Graphic design

Lettering; samples of freehand drawing; examples of work showing page layout; projects related to advertising, publicity or packaging; typography; work completed to a brief, such as a complete publicity campaign for a product; digitally manipulated images; evidence that you read design magazines and visit exhibitions.

Illustration

Work done from direct observation; work related to a design and technology project (if applying for technical or scientific illustration courses); work done to a 'brief' – for example, a piece done to illustrate pages of a particular book, with sample text and notes explaining how you set out to emphasise particular aspects; evidence that you read appropriate literature and visit exhibitions.

Product design

Drawings, diagrams, computer-aided designs; working notes, showing that you understand the workshop processes necessary to manufacture the product; preliminary sketches; photographs of the finished article; evidence that you read design magazines and visit exhibitions.

Guidance on portfolio preparation for specialist courses

> *'Interviews are an opportunity for you to demonstrate your commitment and self-motivation to a chosen area of study, and to discuss aspects of your chosen course and ask any questions that you may have. You will be expected to display and discuss your portfolio. Portfolios should contain examples of work (both finished and in progress) that showcase your particular interests – not only course or school work, but also any independent work, including for example sketchbooks and any other evidence of your ideas, your interests and passion for your chosen area of study.*
>
> *'The form of portfolio work desired would vary according to the area of study. For example, the BA (Hons) Costume course would require extensive evidence of figurative drawing whereas the BA*

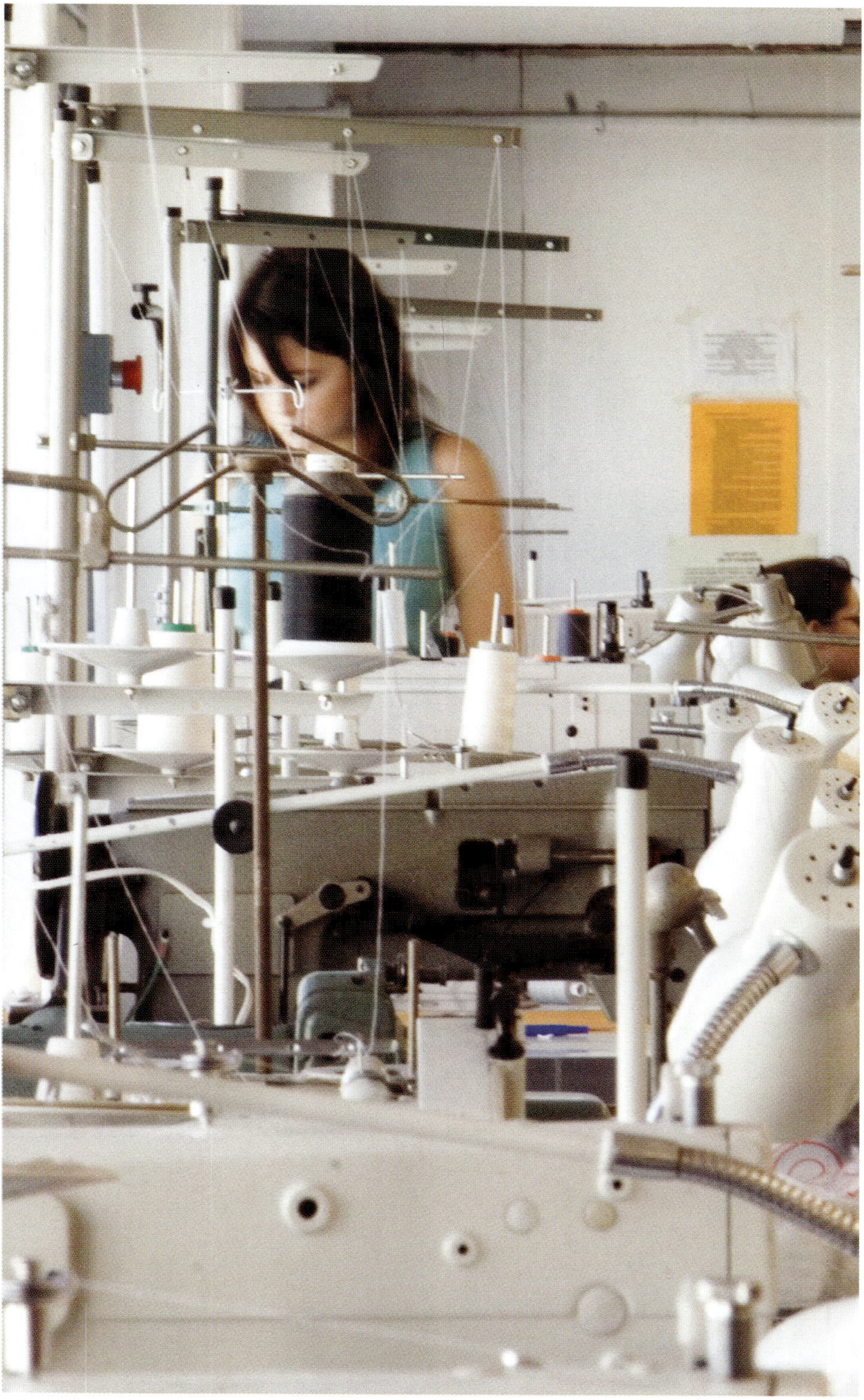

Plate 1 Fashion studios at Winchester School of Art.

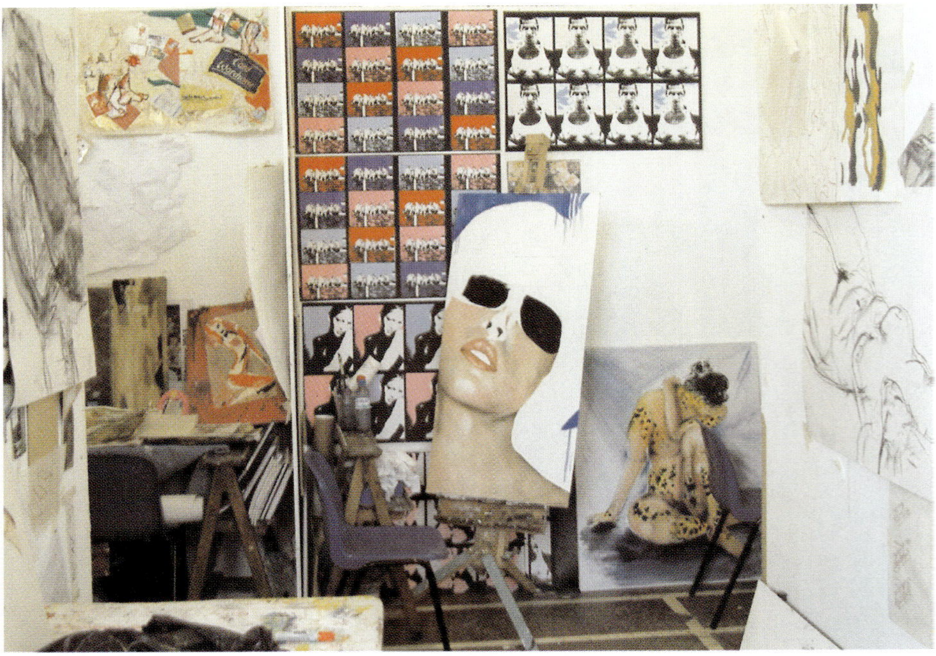

Plate 2 Foundation course projects, Norwich School of Art and Design.

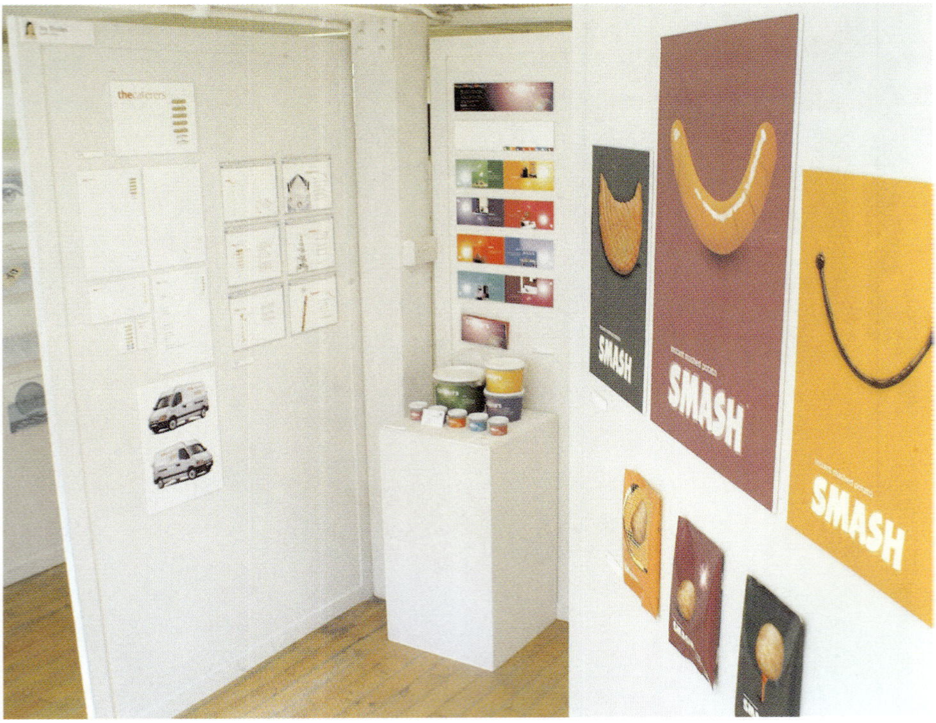

Plate 3 Graphics show, Norwich School of Art and Design.

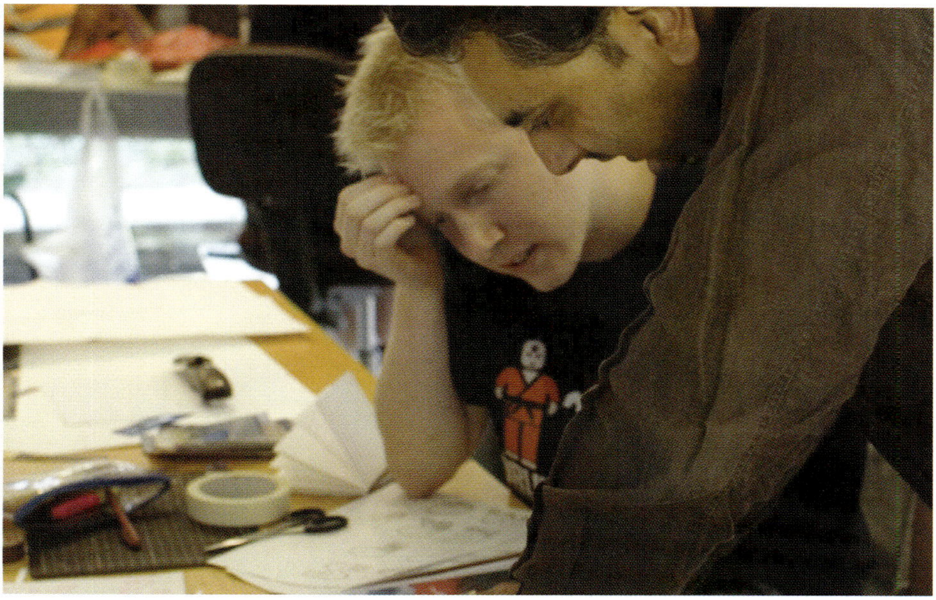

Plate 4 Support from a tutor in the Graphics Arts Studios, Winchester School of Art.

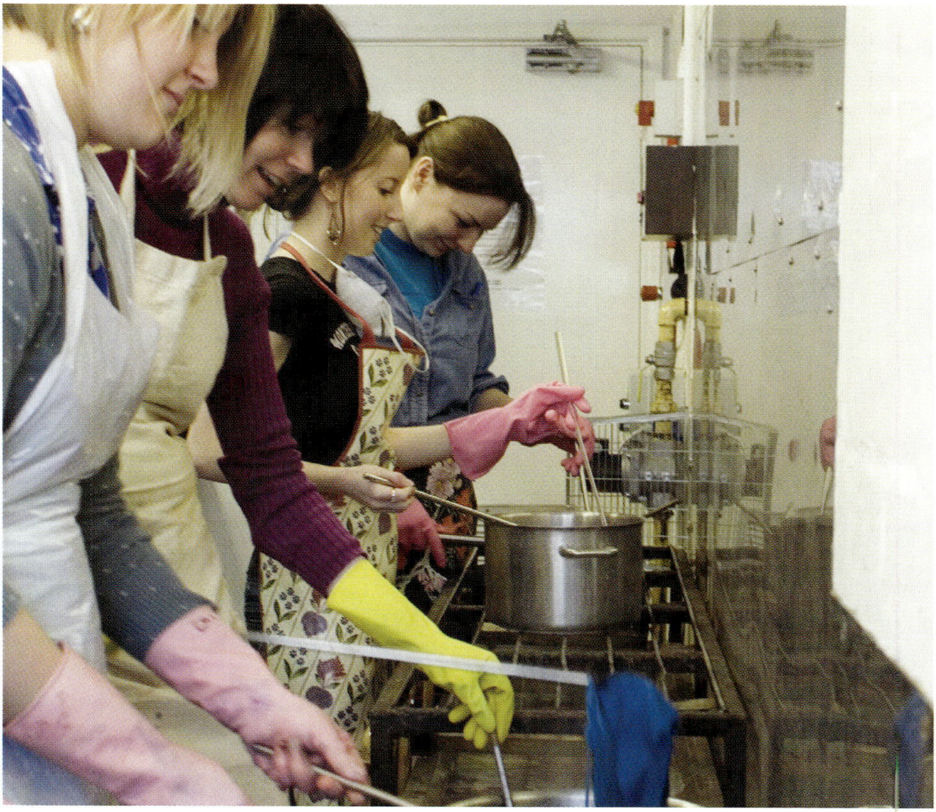

Plate 5 Textiles students in the dye lab at Winchester School of Art.

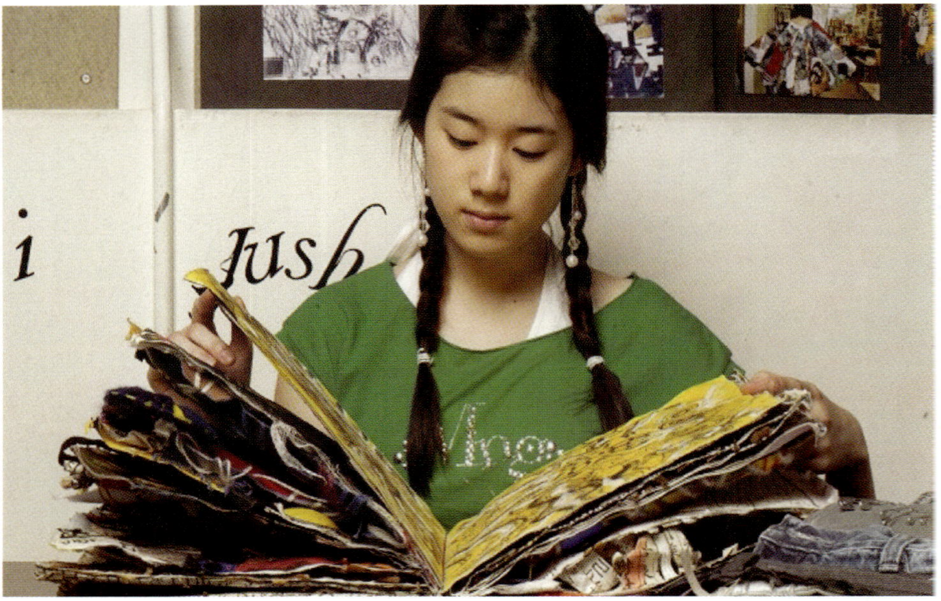

Plate 6 An applicant for the University of the Arts London with her porfolio.

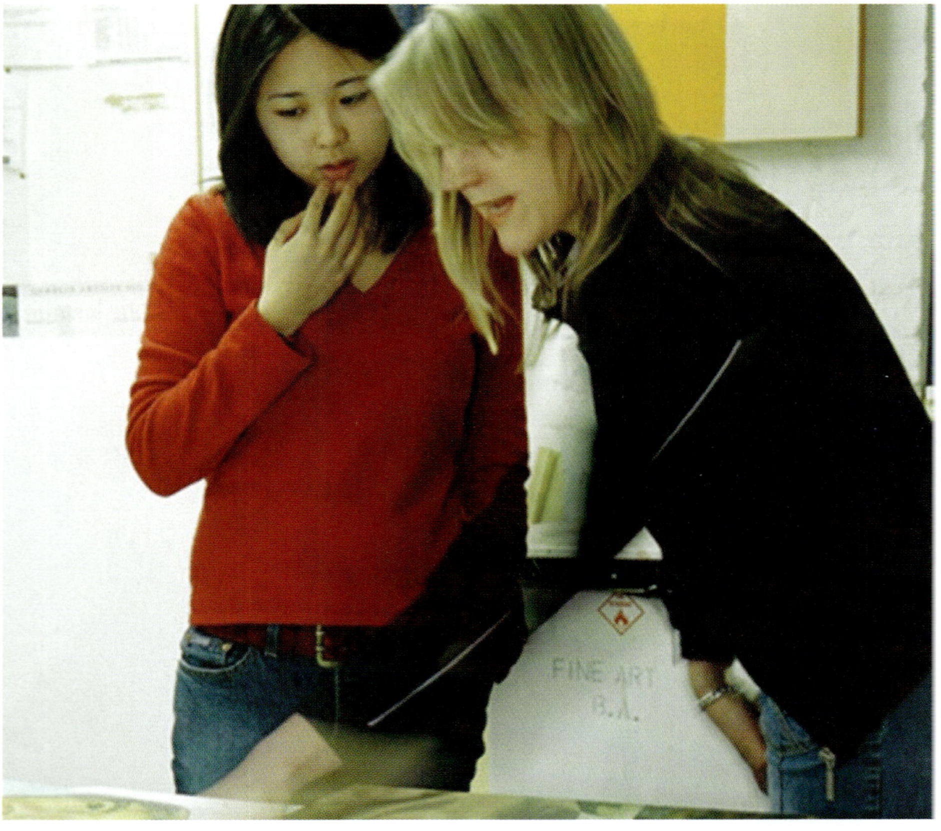

Plate 7 Critique and evaluation is an important part of the learning process at the University of the Arts London.

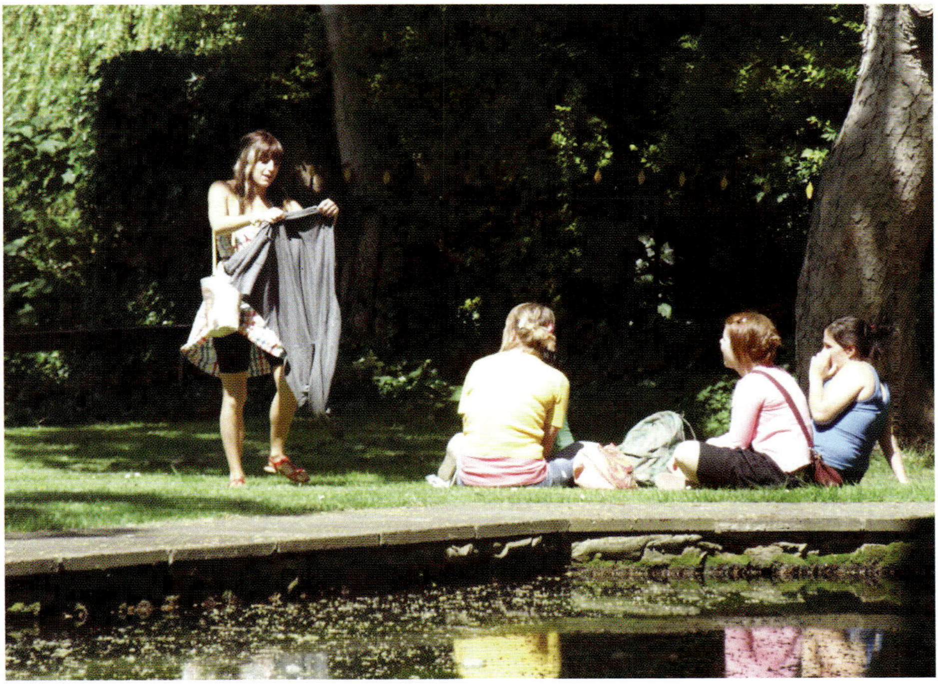

Plate 8 Students taking a break at Winchester School of Art.

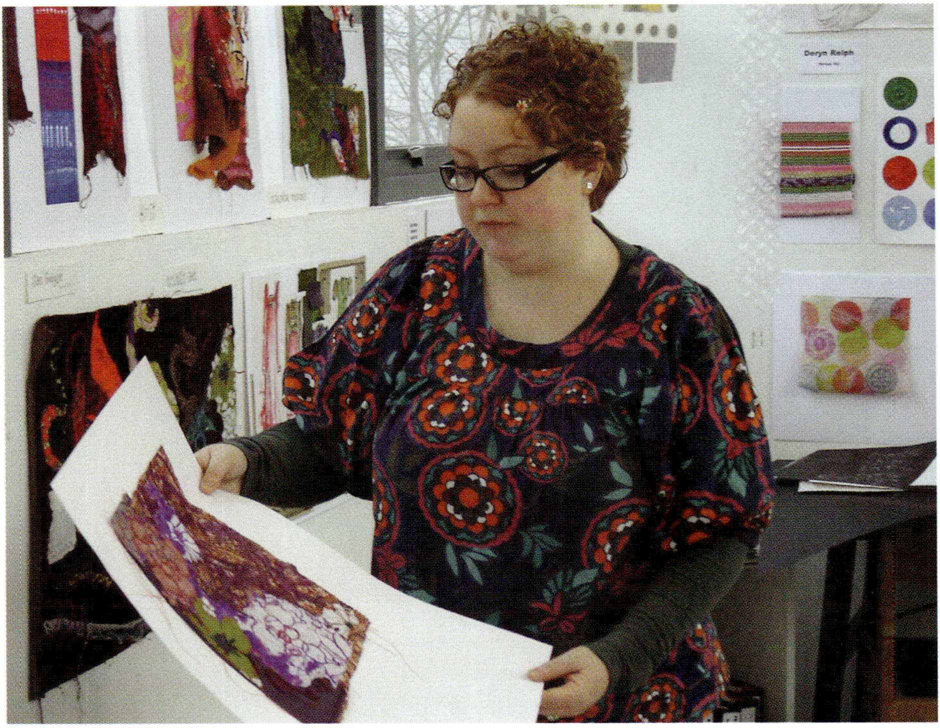

Plate 9 Portfolio interviews are a key part of Winchester School of Art's application process.

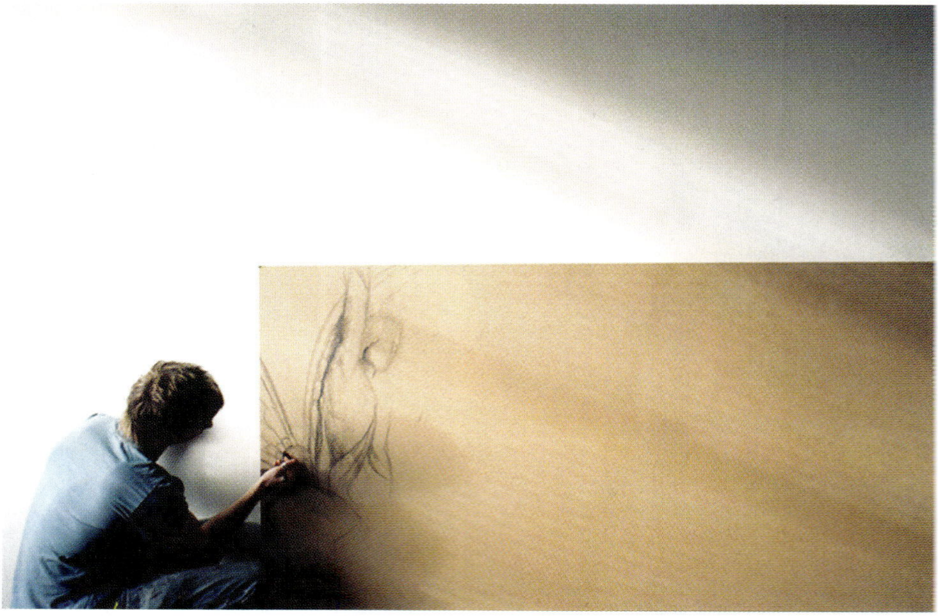

Plate 10 Printmaking facilities at Winchester School of Art Include screenprinting, lithography and etching.

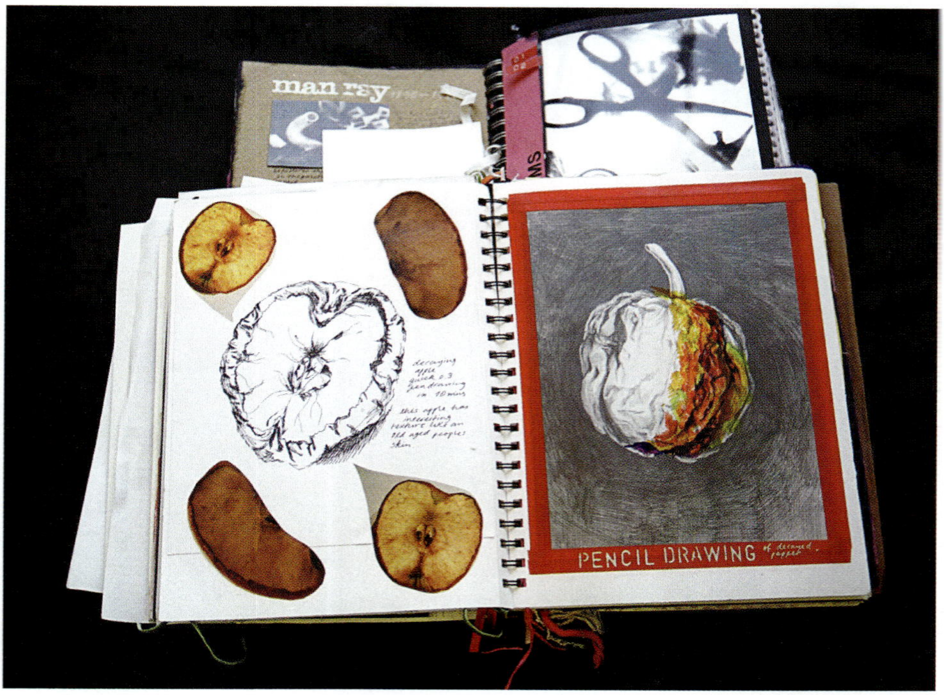

Plate 11 Student sketchbooks.

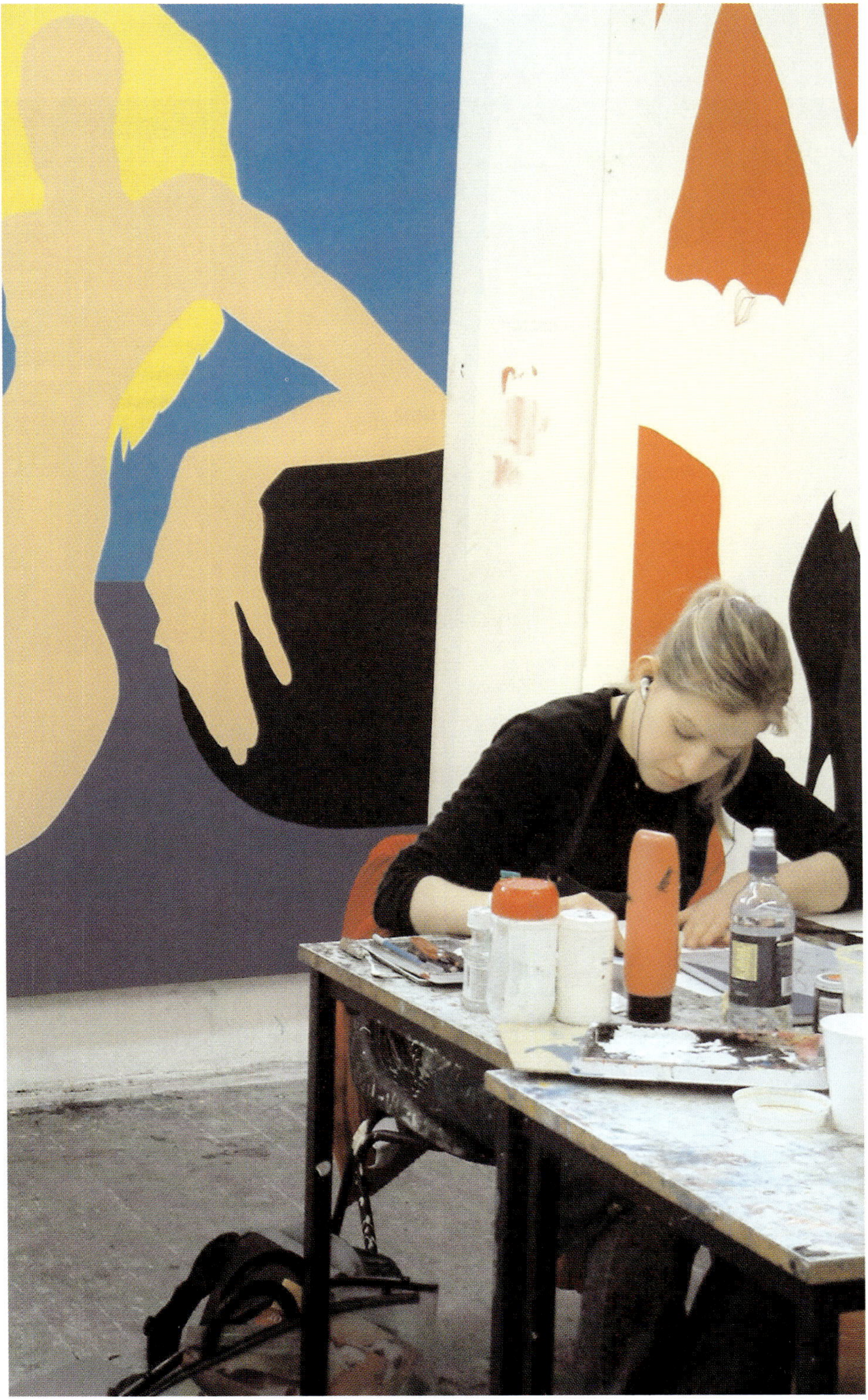

Plate 12 Fine Art studio, Norwich School of Art and Design.

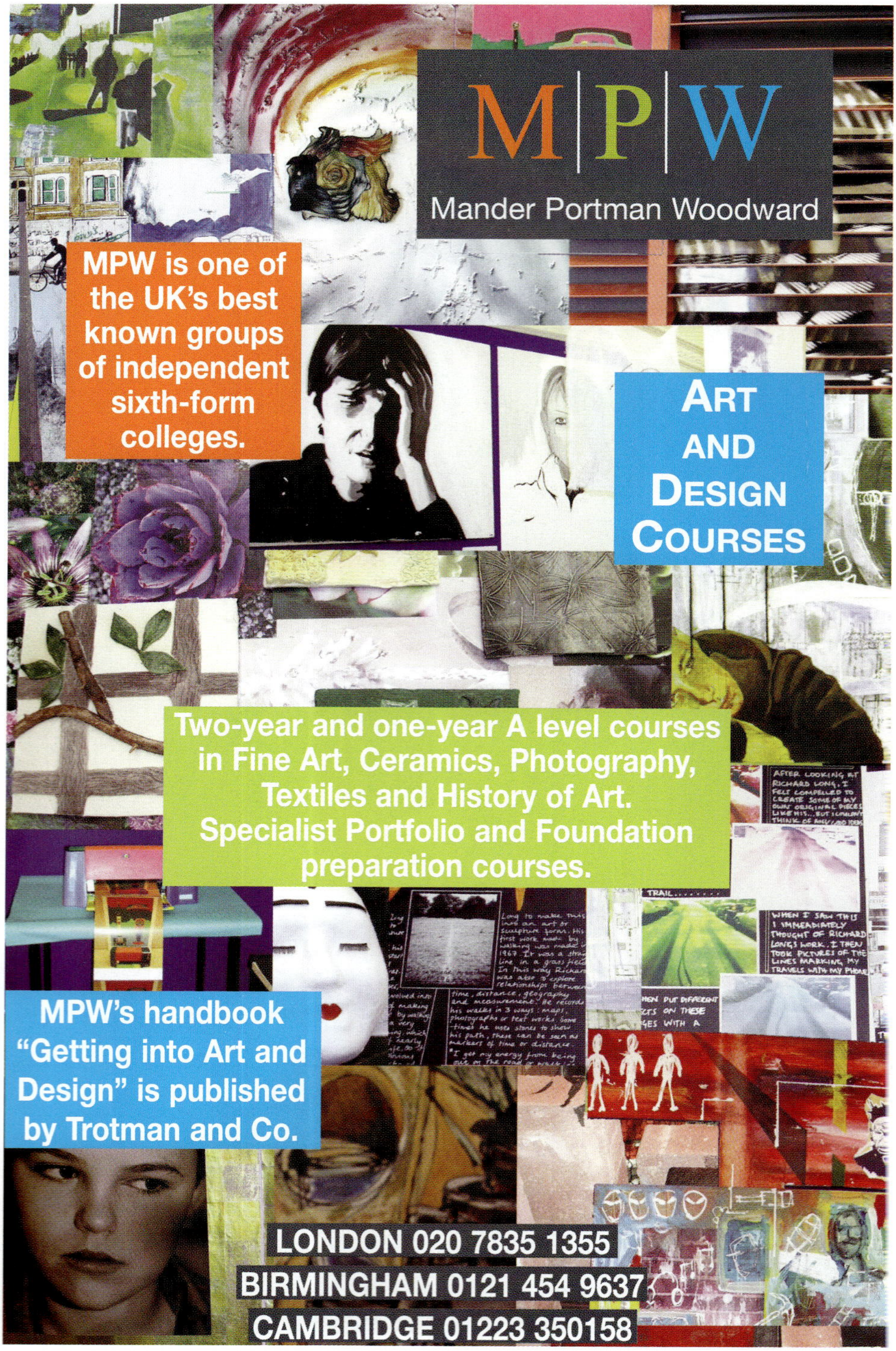
MPW
Mander Portman Woodward
MPW is one of the UK's best known groups of independent sixth-form colleges.
Art and Design Courses
Two-year and one-year A level courses in Fine Art, Ceramics, Photography, Textiles and History of Art. Specialist Portfolio and Foundation preparation courses.
MPW's handbook "Getting into Art and Design" is published by Trotman and Co.
LONDON 020 7835 1355
BIRMINGHAM 0121 454 9637
CAMBRIDGE 01223 350158

(Hons) Model making would require that you show items that you have made, whether in pottery, wood or fabric. The common requirement across the board of courses is that you show evidence of your commitment to your area of study and an ability to visually express your ideas and concepts and show the creative development of your artwork from start to finish. The creative process is an important feature rather than the outcome. Passion for your chosen area of study is also essential as well as the ability to demonstrate and show your potential within a variety of artwork pieces.'

Astrid MacKellar
Arts Institute at Bournemouth

- *'Drawing: evidence of life drawing can be useful because it demonstrates such a particular discipline, but any drawing that shows you can observe and interpret the world around you is important. Drawings can be any scale and in any medium, but a diversity of approaches shows exploration and a keenness to experiment.*
- *Problem solving: your ability to solve visual problems can be demonstrated through design sheets or sketchbooks, but should show in detail how you would deal with design briefs or your own (if more fine art-based) issues or ideas. If anything, these are the most revealing parts of the interview, and for many staff it is more important than seeing finished pieces.*
- *Diversity: a diversity of work and a willingness to experiment are crucial. A good problem solver needs to use any number of techniques and approaches, so you must show flexibility and adaptability. If you come with only one method of working, your methods will look narrow and limited.*
- *Consistency: as well as diversity you need to show that you can also take an idea and "run with it"; that you have developed, in some depth, one or more particular projects or themes.*
- *Independence: at degree level you will need to be able to generate work that is self-directed and independent. Your portfolio, therefore, needs to show that you have developed your own ways of working that haven't been directed solely by your tutors.*
- *Critical/contextual studies: most degree courses have a theoretical element, usually involving written work, so something that shows your ability to write is also important. Interviewers will also need to know that you are interested in the broader context of art and design. You will be asked about practitioners who have influenced or impressed you and exhibitions you've recently visited.*

'Finally, it is impossible to quantify the amount and type of work to take to an interview. While you should include a full range of work that isn't over edited, you should select carefully rather than include absolutely everything you've ever made! Emphasise your most recent work as this is the work that best represents your current concerns. Because it is fresh in your mind this is also the work you'll be able to talk about with the most enthusiasm.

'The key to your portfolio is its organisation. Have a strong beginning and end, and order your work coherently in projects or subjects, giving most emphasis to recent work. Listen to advice from tutors: they have great expertise in helping students gain university places. For three-dimensional or large-scale work, bring good-quality photographs or slides. Better still, bring originals, but good reproductions will often suffice.'

Sarah Horton
BA (Hons) Course Leader
Norwich School of Art and Design

'Ideally, we would like to see a portfolio that demonstrates a high level of visual skill, creativity, commitment and self-motivation. We would be looking for evidence of intellectual enquiry and cultural awareness. We would expect you to have completed a Foundation course and the resulting portfolio may include sketchbooks, ideas books, set projects, self-initiated work, finished pieces, work in progress, photographs, or three-dimensional work. We value a portfolio of work that includes continuity of ideas, and a series of related images that relate to each other in some way. We are interested in your research, thinking and projects that show the development and progression of an idea. We particularly value self-initiated work because it tells us so much about you! Your portfolio should be self-explanatory – it may be viewed initially in your absence! Edit your work and play with the sequencing of images and projects until they unfold in such a way that they tell us who you are, and what you think. And above all we are looking for potential.'

Debbie Cook
Tutor at the Royal College of Art and
International Postgraduate Coordinator
Central St Martins

'A portfolio should speak for itself and tell us about your ideas, your passions and your personal approach to working. A

commitment to the subject and an engagement with projects should be evident. You need to be self-motivated and have the capacity to work independently and this should be reflected in your portfolio. We are interested in the journey your work takes, your ability to recognise and generate ideas, explore their possibilities and develop them. This process of thinking and working, within a broad cultural context, is crucial. Finally, present your work in a clear and organised way to ensure that it communicates all that you want it to.'

Annette Bellwood
International Academic Coordinator
London College of Communication

'Work within your portfolio should reflect your individual identity and should show creative thinking and investigation. You should include work that reveals your capacity to develop a project through all stages from start to finish. In addition, your portfolio should demonstrate the ability to explore different approaches and solutions to art and design challenges. You can include sketch-books, notebooks and contact sheets as well as finished work.'

University of the Creative Arts Prospectus

'The admissions panels will pay particular attention to candidates' notebooks/sketchbooks, especially with regard to the extent to which they reflect the range of a candidate's interests and experience. Notebooks/sketchbooks are regarded as being of great value in recording images and exploring ideas. Sketchbooks should illustrate the investigation and research process through sketches, drawings, collage and colour studies, they should not simply be scrapbooks. Notebooks and sketchbooks are a very important part of your portfolio. They tell us what you are looking at and how you are looking at it.'

Edinburgh College of Art website

'As soon as your portfolio is opened it must capture attention. To help you achieve this, here are some general guidelines.

- *Preparation: be prepared to adapt the portfolio according to the course you are applying to (just like you would a CV or personal statement).*
- *Sequence: the portfolio should be well organised – so that whoever looks through it understands how you develop your ideas and how you move from one idea to the next. Also include notebooks and sketchbooks.*

- *Scope: show the range of what you can do, concentrating on recent work. Include visual and other background research, sketches, models and prototypes – not just the finished work.*
- *Context: it should show whatever interests you, and how it influences the work you are passionate about – fashion, music, sport, and environment … whatever.*
- *Selection: be choosy; pick work that shows ideas, skills and media which you want to explore further in the course that you would like to do. Don't include too much and avoid repetition of one kind of work just because you think you are good at it. Generally 15 to 20 items for a portfolio should be enough.'*

Hereford College of Art and Design website

'Sketchbooks are extremely important. They should be a "diary" of your thinking and include observational and speculative drawings/sketches communicating a visual sensitivity. We also look for evidence of how you develop and work through your ideas. Include photographs and collected images, however avoid your sketchbooks becoming merely scrapbooks.'

Middlesex University website

WARNING!

On no account even consider 'borrowing' someone else's work for your portfolio. As well as being unethical, you are almost certain to be found out, as the differences of style will be quite obvious to the trained eyes of the interviewers.

Checklist

- ☐ Round up your work
- ☐ Check out portfolio specification
- ☐ Purchase portfolio
- ☐ Attend evening classes
- ☐ Review portfolio
- ☐ Set targets and deadlines
- ☐ Photograph three-dimensional work
- ☐ Label portfolio
- ☐ Adapt portfolio to particular specification

06 The interview

This chapter is about how to make the most of your interview. Although the format of the interview will vary from college to college and there are differences between interviewing for a Foundation course and a specialist degree course, the following guidelines will be of help to you. Make sure that you read this chapter in conjunction with Chapter 5.

What is the purpose of the interview?

Interviews are there to help art schools find the most appropriate students and to help students find the most appropriate art schools. Most people who fear interviews do so either because they misunderstand their purpose or because they do not know what to expect and imagine the worst. We worry that we will be asked impossible questions, that the interviewers will not like us or that they will try to catch us out; we worry that we will not be good enough.

Consider this: art schools exist because students want to study art and design. Without the students there would be no colleges, no lecturers, no admissions tutors and no courses. In other words, where would art schools be without you? You are the single most important element in the educational process and, as such, it is not in any college's interest to make life difficult for you. Yes, interviewers will be trying to find out whether you are suited to the course for which you are applying and, yes, they will be carefully considering both you and your work and, yes, you can expect to be asked some challenging questions – but try to take a positive attitude. Most people are nervous at interview; admissions tutors understand this and will make allowances. They are there to get the best from you.

Also, remember that the interview provides you with an opportunity to assess a prospective college. Hopefully, you will have visited the college before your interview and checked things out, but a second look around will not do you any harm. Since you will probably be studying under some of the people who will be interviewing you, check them out too.

What to expect

In some colleges you deliver your portfolio for consideration prior to being offered an interview. At others, you leave it with the admissions tutors on the day of your interview. They will initially look at it without you and then ask you in to discuss it with them. This can happen 10 minutes after they take it or sometimes later that day. In many instances, especially at interviews for degree courses, you begin your interview by being asked to present your work briefly to an interviewer or a panel of interviewers who are seeing it for the first time. In many cases, a conversation begins as you show your work, developing into a more formal question-and-answer session towards the end of the interview. However, interviews vary from college to college, so before attending read through the college's literature to find out what the format will be.

Interviews vary in length from as little as five or 10 minutes to up to 30 or 40 minutes for specialist degree courses. Do not be surprised or worried if the interview feels as if it was very short. Time seems to pass much more rapidly in this kind of situation. Also remember that the interviewers are experts, know what they are looking for and often will be able to come to a decision quickly. This is particularly the case for Foundation courses where admissions tutors will frequently have to see literally hundreds of students in a matter of weeks.

In some cases you will find out if you have been successful on the day, but in most you will be notified by post in due course.

Preparing

It is impossible to know exactly what you will be asked at interview, and in some ways it is not helpful to be overly prepared since it is much better to allow a discussion to develop naturally, answering the questions that you have been asked rather than insisting that you talk about what you have been reading up on. However, while being over-prepared is one thing, being under-prepared is quite another and should be avoided at all costs – it will suggest to the interviewers that you are not really interested in the course. The best way to prepare is to think in general about how you might respond to the specific questions you know that you are likely to be asked. As a guide consider the following.

- Why have you applied for this particular course?
- Why have you applied to study it here?
- Which artists have influenced you?
- What are you hoping to do in the future?

If you have been conscientious about choosing a course, you will be able to make a positive response to the first two questions. (Make sure that you have read Chapters 1 and 2.) Rereading your notes, looking through the course prospectus and talking things through with others will all help. Rather than trying to 'revise' for the answers that you think the interviewers will want, simply remind yourself of what you have done, so that you can respond honestly.

With respect to the question 'Which artists have influenced you?', before going to the interview look through your work and consider how it relates to that of others. If you have worked on a written project, reread it. Looking through your sketchbooks can also help, since they are, in part, a record of your creative process. You will probably have collected cuttings and postcards. These visual prompts will help to remind you of your influences.

During the period leading up to your interview, make a point of getting out and about. Make sure that you visit some exhibitions. In addition to looking at well-known exhibits in museums, go and see a show of new work. Also keep up to date by reading the arts pages of national newspapers and periodicals – see the reading list in Chapter 12. If you are applying for a place on a Foundation course it is likely that your future plans will include taking a degree. You can say this. If you are applying for a place on a specialist degree course, jotting down a few notes to help you think things through may be helpful in preparing for the fourth question on page 58. Whatever your thoughts might be, do not worry if you cannot come up with a complete answer. That is perfectly normal. It would be a pretty boring world to live in if we all knew exactly what we were going to do in the future! You just need to be able to show the interviewer that you are reflecting on your options and have some possible ideas in mind.

Assuming that you have done your homework and know as much as possible about the course, you will not need to use up valuable time asking questions about course structure or discussing specific issues such as funding. If you are given the chance to ask questions or make comments, it is usually much better to respond to something you have just been discussing with the interviewer than to set your own agenda.

Perhaps the best way to prepare for this is by taking a mock interview, which will give you a feel for how an interview develops. Many schools and colleges offer mock interviews to their own students and in some cases to external candidates. If you have the chance to do one, make sure you do not miss out. Mock interviews provide excellent preparation and an excellent way to identify and resolve potential problems.

Discussing your work with art college or university teachers can be a daunting prospect and you will need to practise before your interview. As a general rule of thumb, try to structure any discussion of your work as follows.

- **Where the idea for the piece came from.** This is an opportunity to talk about artists whose work you like, exhibitions you have visited or previous work that you have produced.
- **How your ideas were realised in the piece.** You could talk about the composition, the materials and the techniques you used as well as what the work represents.
- **Where the work will lead you.** You could talk about what you will work on next, what you might have done differently or how the piece has led you to investigate other artists or techniques.

The interviewer will help you by asking you questions and possibly suggesting other areas of research.

Practicalities

As well as thinking about the kind of questions that you might be asked, it is also important to consider a few practicalities. For example, how will you be travelling to the interview? If you are applying to a local art school you may only have to make a short journey. On the other hand, you may be applying to a course a long way from home, so consider the logistics. In some cases an overnight stay may be necessary.

Also think about how you intend to transport your work. In many instances you will be able to carry everything in a portfolio. As has been mentioned, most colleges are happy to look at photographs of three-dimensional or larger pieces. However, in some situations (e.g. with pieces under a certain size) it will be necessary to take this work with you. You may need to ask a friend for help or to ask the college for advice.

Practise your presentation technique. Can you comfortably manage your portfolio or is it too heavy?

The night before

Assuming that you are well organised, there should be nothing left to do except relax and get a good night's sleep, so make sure that you do! Easy to say, but difficult to do. We all get nervous before a big day and you might find it difficult to switch off. Don't worry if this happens – it just means that you're normal. Try doing something to take your mind off things, like watching a film, chatting with friends or maybe taking a little gentle exercise, and try not to worry. Be positive. Remember, art schools cannot exist without students!

The interview itself: some tips

- **Make sure you arrive early.** You do not want to be rushing around at the last minute.
- **Dress comfortably.** Your interviewers will be far more interested in who you are and what you do than what you wear. If your hair is bright blue and shaved on one side, fine. If it is not, well that is fine too. You will need much more than a good hairstyle to get into art school!
- **Make eye contact.** If you are asked to show your work, make sure that you do not turn your back on the interviewers. Try to position your portfolio between yourself and the people you are speaking to or, if you are standing side by side, turn towards them from time to time.
- **Be willing to listen as well as talk.** Sometimes when we are nervous we talk too much. Try to listen carefully to the questions that you are being asked. You will respond far more intelligently if you understand what has been said. If you do not understand, do not be afraid to ask for further explanation. Sometimes there will be pauses in the conversation. Do not let this unnerve you: the tutors are just concentrating while they look at your work.
- **Afterwards be willing to consider new ideas.** You will be very difficult to teach if you find it hard to keep an open mind. Try not to become defensive if some of your responses to questions are challenged.
- **Be yourself.** You do not need to put on an act; never try to bluff or lie. You will always be found out, so only show your own work and if you do not know something then say so.
- **Above all, be enthusiastic**. Do not be afraid to express your commitment and passion for your subject. You will have worked very hard up to this point. Let your interviewers know that this matters to you. Try not to be cool. Art schools are looking for motivated students.

Hope

Use the acronym HOPE as a reminder of the personal qualities that you will try to display at interview:

- honesty
- open-mindedness

- preparedness
- enthusiasm.

Meet up with a friend and talk things through: this will help you to put things into perspective. Also it will greatly help your fellow students if you give them some feedback. They may not have had an interview yet and your experience will be beneficial. A day or two later, when you have had the chance to reflect a little, make a note of anything that sticks in your mind that might be helpful for next time.

> *'I was expecting to be asked a lot of difficult questions about why I had chosen CSM and about why they should choose me, but in fact the interview was very friendly, more like a chat than an interview. Most of the questions were about my portfolio and I spent a lot of time talking about my work and my interests, and about exhibitions I had visited. I got some feedback from the interviewer, through my referee: apparently, I was "very talkative"! I think that this was because I was nervous, but also because the interviewer made me feel relaxed. It worked though, as I was offered a place.'*

Evelyn Lu
Foundation course student
Central St Martins

> *'The hardest thing about my Camberwell interview was having the confidence to talk about my own work in front of the interviewer, who was a teacher there, and I knew that every day he would be seeing work from so many talented students. I kept thinking that he would find my work uninteresting and my ideas juvenile and naive. He could see I was nervous and so he was reassuring and tried to encourage me. He reacted to some of the things I said as if he was very excited by my ideas, which he probably wasn't, but it made me feel better and so I talked more. I came away feeling quite hopeful, and I was ecstatic when I got my offer of a place.'*

Martin Lee
Foundation course student
Camberwell College of Arts

> *'Before my interview, my art teacher said to me, "You cannot draw as well as Leonardo da Vinci, create sculptures like Rodin, use colour like Howard Hodgkin, or have Antony Gormley's ability to turn an idea into something inspirational. But your interviewers are not looking for fully realised abilities. They are looking for creativity and a willingness to experiment: and you*

have these qualities. So go into the interview determined to show them this."'

Vicky
Foundation student
Chelsea College of Art

Tutors' advice: Foundation courses

'In interview, the reviewers are looking for students who demonstrate curiosity about why the world looks like it does. One expects the beginning of an interest in and knowledge of art and design; the context of art and design. Who does art and design and why? What magazines, books and TV programmes is a student interested in and why? Have they ever visited a museum, gallery, film or concert on their own without the prompting of school, college or friends? Can they name a living designer or architect? What has been the most striking visual experience they have had in the last year? Answers to these questions reveal whether a student's education has led them passively to this point or whether they have a genuine desire for discovery.'

Bill Watson
International Coordinator
Camberwell College of Arts

'Students are normally interviewed by me or another experienced member of the department staff. We spend between 20 and 30 minutes with each applicant. During this time we expect them to talk through their portfolio, which we will normally have looked at in advance and will ask questions about. Interview questions focus on both how and why the work was produced and how it might develop, and on wider issues – for example, on the applicant's interest in the work of other designers or artists. I will expect them to be able to talk about books, journals and shows, and to be able to get under the skin of a subject. I want to know what they have read that is related to art and design – like Art Monthly, Creative Review, Design Week *or* Frieze. *Can they talk about favourite artists and designers? Have they done any research in their own time? Visited galleries and exhibitions? It is not always possible for students who live miles from a large town or city to make many live visits but anyone can use the internet and do some research there. They could also ask if they could have reading rights at their local art school library. Many will say yes, even though they probably will not*

allow them to borrow books. All these activities show evidence of initiative – which course tutors like very much!'

Ros Naylor
Head of Foundation Studies
Winchester School of Art

'At Edinburgh College of Art (ECA), all first choice applicants to the general first year course in Art and Design are invited to bring their portfolio for assessment in March/April.

'Applicants in subsequent rounds of UCAS are only asked to bring portfolios for assessment if places are still available on the course. Applicants are required to submit their portfolio, and their responses to five questions prior to their assessment. At the assessment, you will be asked to pin up a small group of works on a 1.2 square metres wall space. These should be the pieces of work that you consider to be your strongest.

'The five questions are:

1| *Why have you applied to the First Year Studies course in Art and Design at ECA?*
2| *How did you find out about the FYS course at ECA?*
3| *Students of Art and Design at ECA are required to complete courses on the theory, history and criticism of art, design and culture. Why do you think such courses are necessary preparation for potential artists, designers and/or filmmakers?*
4| *What alternative plans do you have if we are unable to offer you a place on the course this year?*
5| *Why do you consider the work you are displaying on the wall above your portfolio to be your strongest?'*

Stella Sinclair
Edinburgh College of Art

'Above all else, you will need to show a seriousness and enthusiasm for your work. Make sure you convince your interviewers that you are passionate about your subject and the particular course you are being interviewed for, as no course leader is interested in a student who lacks energy, enthusiasm and motivation. Also, make sure you know exactly why you are applying for that particular course. Ideally, you will have already visited the college, so talk about that experience.

'Secondly, more than anything else at interview, we are trying to measure potential – your potential to work hard and capacity to

improve. None of this is achievable if you are not open minded. We are interested in students who have a thirst for new ideas and are willing to learn. If you are closed to new ideas it will be impossible to teach you, and your place will be offered to someone else!'

Sarah Horton
BA (Hons) Fine Art Course Leader
Norwich School of Art and Design

'When I meet prospective students, I am looking for potential. Not just artistic ability, but as important, I will look for commitment and enthusiasm. After all, innate talent is only a small element of what it takes to be successful. More often, it is an ability to work hard and a desire to achieve.'

Dr Mary O'Neill
Senior Lecturer in Cultural Context,
Higher Education Academy Teaching Fellow
Faculty of Art Architecture and Design
University of Lincoln

Checklist

- ☐ Visit exhibitions
- ☐ Read arts pages of national newspapers and magazines
- ☐ Review portfolio
- ☐ Conduct a mock interview
- ☐ Check interview date, time and location
- ☐ Find out how to get to interview

07 Architecture

There are a number of possible routes for students who wish to apply for architecture courses. Applications for some courses, such as those offered by art colleges, are made in the same way as for other art and design courses; but you can also apply to study architecture at UCAS institutions without the need to do a Foundation course, or at private institutions. These routes are described in this chapter.

Of all the different manifestations of art and design that we encounter in our daily lives, the work of architects is, along with that of clothes and product designers, the one that people come into contact with most often. Every shop, office building, fast-food outlet, cinema, coffee shop, bridge or multi-storey car park that you see on your way to school or work has been designed by an architect. The work of some architects is immediately recognisable: the 'Bird's Nest' 2008 Olympic stadium in Beijing (a collaboration between Swiss architects and Chinese artistic consultants), the Pompidou Centre, or Frank Gehry's Guggenheim museum in Bilbao spring to mind. But your house or flat was also designed by an architect, as was your tube or bus station.

To practise as an architect in the UK you need to gain registration with the Architects Registration Board (ARB). This takes a minimum of seven years after you leave school. But don't be put off by this if you are interested in architecture because this does not mean that you would spend seven years in lectures: although you will have to attend some lectures, the seven years involves a combination of academic study and work experience in an architectural practice. If you are interested in architecture and want a shorter course so that you can work within the fields of architecture or related subjects such as interior design, then there are other, shorter options available. This chapter will explain the different routes available to you.

Qualifying as an architect

Registration with the ARB

In order to gain registration with the ARB, you need to pass three stages, which are overseen by the Royal Institute of British Architects (RIBA – incidentally, if you are serious about becoming an architect, try to visit the RIBA's London headquarters, which holds many exhibitions as well as being the home to an impressive architecture bookshop). A typical route to gaining registration is shown in Table 1.

Choosing a course

If you are going to embark on the journey towards becoming an architect, you need to think carefully about the first three years of the course. There are a number of options and the right one for you will depend very much on your academic and creative strengths. There are about 40 universities in the UK that offer three- or four-year undergraduate degrees in architecture (usually UCAS code K100) that will give you exemption from RIBA Part 1. There is a section on the RIBA website that lists these institutions (see Chapter 12). Some of these are more geared towards students who are interested in the structural as well as creative aspects of architecture, and these often require A level Mathematics and/or Physics. Other universities concentrate more on the creative aspects of architecture and so require A level Art. In some cases, history of art can be an advantage if the course has a significant focus on the historical side of architecture. (You will often hear people talking about 'the language of architecture': in the same way that there are rules – which of course can be broken – governing the construction of sentences when we speak English, architects use architectural elements in the design of buildings. Some of these are new but often they are based on historical ideas. Just as we mix old and new words in a sentence, architects can mix old and new architectural details in a building.) For entry onto these courses, you will

Table 1 Stages in the architectural student journey

Year	Programme	Stage in the RIBA process
1 2 3	Bachelor degree in Architecture (BA, BArch, BSc or equivalent (see above)	Part 1
4	Work experience	
5 6	Postgraduate study (Dip Arch, MArch or equivalent)	Part 2
7	Work experience	Part 3

be judged on your portfolio as well as on your academic achievements or predictions.

If you are reading this before choosing your A level subjects or equivalent, then spend some time looking at the entrance requirements of university architecture courses to ensure that you will have the right subjects to apply for the type of course that will suit you best. If you are already studying A levels, then you still need to do this research to ensure that you do not waste choices on your UCAS application. The UCAS website Course Search facility is a good starting place as the list of K100 Architecture courses has links through to the universities' entrance requirements. If you are already studying A levels and you are not doing the right subjects for an application to study architecture, you have two options:

1| take an extra year on your A levels, and add the necessary subjects
2| think about following an Access course or an art Foundation course. The universities will be able to advise you on what alternatives to A levels they might be prepared to accept.

Diploma courses

An alternative to the university route described above is offered by the Architectural Association (AA) School of Architecture in London. The AA is, as its name suggests, a specialist architecture school and it offers a Foundation course for students with a limited art background, a three-year course leading to RIBA Part 1, and diploma and master's courses for students wishing to qualify as architects or to pursue postgraduate studies in architecture. The AA programme has multiple entry points, depending on the student's previous experience. Entry to either the Foundation course or the first year of the three-year course is through a combination of academic qualifications (two A levels, one of which must be in an academic subject) and portfolio. Bear in mind that the AA School is a private institution, and so the fee structure differs from that of UCAS institutions. Details on all of the above are available on the AA website (see Chapter 12). See also Chapter 5 for more information on preparing your portfolio.

Preparation for your applications

Architecture courses are oversubscribed. Last year, according to UCAS, there were 5,289 applicants for the 3,786 places available on degree courses; and so it is important to be able to demonstrate to the admissions staff that you are a serious applicant. More than any of the other courses that this book deals with, architecture applicants will benefit enormously from gaining some work experience with an architect before applying to the universities. You can find lists of local architects on the RIBA website (see Chapter 12 for details). In order to make your application as strong as possible, other things you should do prior to the application include:

- reading books on the history of architecture, and on contemporary architecture
- doing some research on the uses of, and properties of, common building materials such as glass, steel, concrete, stone, etc.
- background reading on a favourite building or structure (preferably one you have visited)
- visits to exhibitions
- keeping a small notebook with you, in which you can make notes and sketches on buildings that interest you.

And of course, all these things will be mentioned in your UCAS personal statement.

Alternative architecture courses

Not everyone who has an interest in studying about architecture wants to practise as an architect. There is a whole range of other careers that involve architecture, including:

- administration work in an architectural practice
- architectural model making or computer-aided design
- interior design
- local council planning
- structural engineering
- teaching.

There are several courses other than the K100 degrees mentioned in the previous section that can lead to careers associated with architecture, for example:

- courses at art schools, such as the three-year BA Architecture: Spaces and Objects course at Central St Martins (University of the Arts London)
- engineering-related courses
- art history courses.

Entry into courses such as the one at Central St Martins usually requires the student to have completed an art Foundation course (see Chapter 1).

The personal statement

A personal statement for entry onto an architecture course should incorporate the following sections.

- Why are you applying for architecture?
- What have you done to investigate architecture?
- The relevance of your A levels (or equivalent) or other courses.

Remember, the UCAS form is limited to 4,000 characters.

Personal statement: example 2 (word count 537)

When I was a child, I loved to sketch the houses and streets in my local area. As I grew older, I continued to be fascinated by the building work going on around me and the changing face of the city as I observed modern buildings replacing older ones.

I would love to transform a city through the power of my ideas, such as Gaudi did in Barcelona; or to exhibit at the Design Museum like Zaha Hadid. I have been able to look at the creative aspects of architectural photography through the eyes of Sugimoto and Helene Binet, and I hope that appreciating a more abstract approach to documenting designs will help me to create exciting buildings in the future. Studying physics at A level has helped me to understand the importance of choosing the right materials for structures, and how the development of materials (for example, reinforced concrete) allowed architects to create ever more exciting designs. I have also become interested in how structural elements necessary to stop a building falling down can become beautiful additions to the building, such as the use of flying buttresses in Gothic cathedrals.

At AS level, my history of art course had a large element of architecture, and so I was able to appreciate the links between social and political issues and how they affected developments in architecture. We visited Florence and although we were looking at Renaissance buildings, I found Michelucci's 1935 modernist station, made of iron and glass, the most exciting building we visited.

To investigate architecture further, I spent three weeks last summer work shadowing in a local architectural practice. I used their computer programs to design a family house, and to see how the firm used a model maker to create prototypes of buildings using Perspex. I also became aware of how much paperwork is involved in turning an idea into a practical project, including mastering the many planning laws and requirements, and costing a project. Over the Easter holidays this year I am going to go back there for a further two weeks.

As I live in London, I regularly visit the Architecture Gallery of the V&A museum; I enjoyed the China Design Now exhibition there, which featured architectural projects related to the 2008 Olympic Games. I visit the RIBA often to browse through the books in the bookshop there, as well as seeing the current exhibitions. I particularly enjoyed seeing the exhibition of recent RIBA-award winners. It was fascinating to see how 'green' issues are increasingly playing an important part in the design of new buildings.

When I am not studying, I like to draw. I have been taking evening classes in life drawing, and I spent one week last summer on a print-making workshop. I enjoy music (I play the oboe in the school orchestra, which is extremely useful in learning how to work with others) and I am the treasurer of the school charity society. At the weekend, I have a part-time job in a supermarket where I work on the tills. I deal with all sorts of people, including a few who are unhappy about some aspect of the supermarket, which has helped me learn to stay calm under pressure and to be diplomatic.

WARNING!

Do not copy this personal statement: it is only intended to be a guide.

You will have noticed that the applicant has dropped a number of hints as to what she would like to discuss at the interview, by mentioning buildings, architects and ideas. If she is lucky, her interviewers will be interested in hearing her expand on these ideas, and so she will be able to talk about things she has already prepared. For example, she has mentioned:

- Gaudi
- Zaha Hadid
- Sugimoto
- Helene Binet
- use of reinforced concrete
- Gothic architecture
- Florence and the railway station

- links between social and political issues in relation to architecture
- exhibitions at the V&A and the RIBA
- 'green' issues
- her work experience.

Of course, in order to impress her interviewers, she would need to do a good deal of research into the things she has touched on in the personal statement. If there is one thing guaranteed to create a bad impression at the interview, it is being unable to talk about things in the personal statement.

> *'I was not confident about getting a place at the AA because I knew the competition for places was great, so I was surprised when I got an interview. At the interview, I tried my best to explain my work, and fortunately I was asked the question I was expecting: why I wanted to study at the AA. I brought along an architectural model I had made at school, in art, and I explained that it could be seen as a pavilion. Then one interviewer asked me "What is a pavilion?" At that point I became more and more anxious and nervous, and started using the wrong words and forgot what I had prepared. I was asked about my sketchbooks, and about why my textiles, art and photography books looked similar, but I tried to justify this by saying that all these subjects belong to art. But I really felt that I would be rejected, so it was with great excitement that I discovered not only that I had been offered a place but also that it was for the first year of the course rather than the Foundation.'*

Ding (Rainbow) Ni
Year 1 student
Architectural Association School of Architecture

08 Offers

Foundation courses

In most cases, any offer you receive will be unconditional. In other words, the college has been convinced by your portfolio and interview, and they want you. All you have to do then is to decide whether you want them! However, please note that in nearly all cases you will be expected to complete your current programme of study successfully.

Conditional offers

Under some circumstances you might be made a conditional offer. This normally happens because the college feels that while your work is promising you are not yet ready to cope with the demands of a Foundation course, because they require a particular A level grade or because as an overseas student you would benefit from help with your language skills or with adapting to UK teaching methods in general. In this situation you may be asked to attend a summer course. (There is a charge for these courses.)

Accepting an offer

Since there is no centralised system for Foundation course applications (other than local schemes such as that run by the University of the Arts London) it is possible to hold a number of offers simultaneously. In this situation, the best strategy is to keep things simple, and not to try to juggle too many balls at one time. When you applied, you had probably already decided which college was your first choice, which was second, and so on. If you are lucky enough to get offers from a number of colleges, stick to your original plan and accept the offer from the place where you most want to study. Do not accept offers from everyone just to keep your options open. Talk to your teachers or careers advisers if you are unsure about your best course of action.

Degree courses

You may receive an offer directly from the art school to which you have applied or, if you are applying through UCAS, you will (if all goes to plan) receive offers from more than one college. If you are lucky, these will be unconditional offers (which means that the offer does not depend on your achieving specific grades).

Conditional offers

If you receive a conditional offer, it will specify what the college requires of you – for instance, it may ask for a good grade in A level Art or, more commonly, good grades in other subjects, particularly if you are going to study for a combined honours degree.

Accepting an offer

When you have received replies from all of your five choices, you will (if you are lucky) be faced with a choice of institutions or courses. You will have to decide which course you want to hold as your firm choice (either conditional – CF, or unconditional – UF) and which you want as your insurance offer (either conditional – CI, or unconditional – UI). The insurance offer is usually a course which requires lower grades or marks than the firm choice. Once you have heard from all five choices, UCAS will send you a summary of their responses and give you a deadline (usually of about one month) in which to make the choice of the firm and insurance offers.

Clearing and Extra

If you are unsuccessful, either because you are not made any offers, or because you do not meet the conditions of your conditional offers,

Table 2 Timetable for UCAS Extra and Clearing

UCAS Extra	Starts end of February	For candidates who have applied through UCAS but have received rejections from all 5 choices. Using the online Track facility, students can approach other institutions, one at a time. Institutions that offer courses through Extra list these on the UCAS website.
Clearing	Starts on A level results day (mid-August)	Candidates who are not holding offers, or have failed to achieve the grades required for their conditional offers can approach other institutions. Course vacancies are listed in the national press and on the UCAS website.

you are eligible to enter Clearing. The Clearing period begins in mid-August. This system means that you can contact other colleges and make new applications. UCAS has also introduced a system called Extra. This starts in March, and allows candidates who are not holding any offers to approach other art schools. For details of both, look at the UCAS website.

What to do if you do not get an offer

Four words: **Do not give up.**

There are many options open to you. For degree applications, there are the Clearing and Extra systems (see above and www.ucas.com). For Foundation courses, you have the option of making direct contact with other colleges. You should also contact the colleges that rejected you to try to get their advice. It may be that they spotted a weakness in a particular area of your work and might be able to give you advice. If you can convince them that you desperately want to come to them and that you will work on that area – by taking evening classes, for example – they might allow you to bring in your updated portfolio later on in the year for reassessment.

If all else fails, you could consider taking a gap year during which you could work on your portfolio to strengthen it. Many colleges offer portfolio courses specifically for this purpose. These are generally part-time and can be on a 1:1 basis or in small groups. In some cases, students are recommended to take a new A level (for example, photography or textiles) and study this on a one-year part-time course, while using their spare time to gain work experience or to enrol on shorter courses that concentrate on, say, life drawing.

09 Fees and funding

Foundation courses

Foundation courses are classed as further education (FE) courses, rather than higher education (HE). For this reason, student loans are not available. However, students from the UK or the EU who are under 19 years old on 31 August in the year that the course starts are eligible for free admission. Students who do not come into this category will have to pay tuition fees, which are likely to be about £800–£1,100 per year for UK/EU students.

Degree and HND courses

All UK and EU students pay tuition fees of up to £3,290 per year (2010 entry) as a contribution towards the cost of the course. Some students will have up to 100% of this paid by their local authority, depending on the income of their parents. Details of how these grants are calculated can be found on the Directgov website (address on page 91). Even if you are not eligible for a grant, your fees do not have to be paid while you are studying – you can take out a loan which does not have to start to be repaid until you are working and earning more than £15,000 per year.

Scottish students who choose a Scottish university or art college do not pay any tuition fees. Welsh students studying in Wales will be charged up to £3,290 a year, but will receive a grant (non-repayable) of up to £1,940 per year to offset the fees. The UCAS website has full details of fees and support arrangements. Students from Northern Ireland who are applying to institutions within Northern Ireland should consult www.studentfinanceni.co.uk for details of what fees they will be expected to pay, and the help that they might receive.

Students on HE courses are eligible to apply for student loans to help with living costs. Students can borrow up to about £10,000 per year.

Postgraduate courses

There is no automatic right to funding or student loans for this type of course. Students are often self-funding – or may be assisted by scholarships from universities or from other organisations. Contacting the institution to which you are applying is a good way to begin exploring your options. See the Appendix at the end of this book for telephone numbers and email addresses.

Other sources of funding

Commercial organisations, charitable trusts, educational institutions and government agencies all offer sponsorship, special grants, access funds and scholarships, but these sources of finance are limited and hard to come by. If you are facing financial difficulties, a good place to start looking for information is the college that you are applying to. For example, University College Falmouth postgraduate students can apply for financial support from Creative Enterprises Cornwall. The college also offers a scholarship in memory of the artist Sandra Blow for a student enrolled on the MA Fine Art: Contemporary Practice course. There are a number of similar sources of support available at institutions throughout the UK. You should look at the 'Funding' sections on the institutions' websites for further information. Remember that these scholarships vary in size and availability from year to year, so you should check the websites regularly for updates.

The Arts and Humanities Research Council (AHRC) also offers some funding for art and design students. Contact details can be found in Chapter 12 of this book.

Contact details for the Student Loans Company (SLC) and for organisations that provide further information on student finance can be found in Chapter 12, and you may also find the *Guide to Student Money 2011* (published by Trotman) a useful read.

International students

Fees for international students range from around £6,500 to £7,500 for Foundation courses, and between £10,000 and £14,000 per year for degree or postgraduate courses. Further details can be found in Chapter 4.

10 Postgraduate courses

Having completed your degree, you can continue your studies, choosing from the wide variety of postgraduate courses that are available. Applications can be made either in the final year of your degree or after you have graduated and completed a period of professional practice.

Types of course

When considering whether or not to apply for postgraduate study your first choice will be between a higher degree, diploma or certificate and then between a taught or research programme. Courses, which vary in structure, include one-, two- and three-year postgraduate degrees, leading, for example, to the award of MA, and postgraduate certificates that prepare students for specific professions, such as a Postgraduate Certificate in Animation, a Diploma in Museum Studies or a PGCE, the teaching qualification. You will also be able to develop a career in research, with a PhD or MPhil (see below for details) being the starting point.

Postgraduate courses are available at many colleges, art schools and universities. Many institutions offer courses at both undergraduate and postgraduate levels, making it possible to remain within the same institution for all your studies. There are also specialist schools of art such as the Royal College of Art and the Royal Academy Schools of Art which offer only postgraduate courses.

Master's degrees

Master's courses used to last for one year and the majority were organised as taught programmes. However, there are now numerous two-year courses. It is now also possible to do a master's degree by research – usually leading to a Master of Philosophy (or MPhil). This is at a higher level than an MA but below that of a doctorate.

Taught master's degrees usually take from nine to 12 months (or two years if you are a part-time student). The first six to nine months are usually studio and classroom based, and are followed by time spent on a research project.

Doctorates

A PhD (Doctor of Philosophy) is always achieved by research under the guidance of a supervisor – a member of academic staff who shares your interest and is an expert in that particular area. Your area of study would be highly specialised and you would have to submit a thesis – of up to 100,000 words – based on original research. A PhD typically takes three years (but can take longer).

Courses cover the full range of art and design disciplines and, while it is usual to continue working within the same area of study that you have followed at undergraduate level, it is also possible to cross over into other areas.

Applying for a postgraduate course

There is no centralised system like UCAS for postgraduate courses, nor is there a set closing date. Some taught programmes have deadlines, but it is often possible to begin a research programme at different points during the academic year. There may, in fact, be different starting dates throughout the year for all types of courses – but the autumn term is still the most popular. There is no limit to the number of applications that you may make, but most students make a maximum of six applications and on average around two to three.

Application procedures vary, but in the first instance you should refer to the college at which you intend to study. You will be required to submit a portfolio, attend an interview and, in some cases, present a formal proposal of an intended programme of study. Take a look at the comments below from Andrew Watson to get an idea of how one college approaches the admissions process.

> *'Postgraduate courses have well-defined portfolio requirements. These will vary in relation to the level of postgraduate study (PG Cert, PG Dip and MA) and in relation to the subject area (design, art, media). Start by checking the published portfolio requirements for the course you are applying to. The portfolio is used as a means of assessing an applicant's suitability for the level of study and their motivation and potential to achieve the course aims and learning outcomes. At postgraduate level you should be able to demonstrate intelligence and maturity of approach to a personal area of interest as well as confidence in the abilities that you will require to explore a range of technical and formal problems. You*

should also emphasise your ability to undertake independent research. For design-based studies it is important to show that you can produce, communicate and evaluate a range of ideas and design responses to a particular problem. MA applicants should be able to show critical and analytical abilities and evidence of original thinking. Fine art and media courses would expect the applicant to be able to show, either at interview or in an accompanying statement, an awareness of the cultural and social context of the work submitted in the portfolio.

'Many courses now limit the quantity and form of the work submitted at application and ask for additional examples to be shown at interview. Again it is very important to check specific published course requirements on this.'

Andrew Watson
PG Cert Professional Studies in Art and Design Course Director
Central St Martins

'I chose the course because it offered me a chance to gain a formal qualification in photography in an environment that was perhaps more practical than theoretical, and to work on and develop personal projects. The other people on the course came from a huge variety of backgrounds and experiences; from practising professional photographers to people who were hoping to change careers. This made the course very stimulating because they all brought their own experiences to the tutorials and group discussions.

'Setting up the final show, Group Photo, was stressful because of the tight deadlines, but it gave me the confidence to exhibit my work and to articulate my intentions. I now hope to study on an MA course, and to make a living from my photography – things that I would never have seriously contemplated before I started the PG Cert course.'

Justina Burnett
PG Cert in Photography
Central St Martins

WARNING!

Funding for these courses is often even harder won than the places gained on them. Once again, contacting the institution to which you are applying is a good way to begin exploring your options. See the Appendix for email addresses and telephone numbers.

11 Careers in art and design

Wherever you are right now, take a look around you. Look closely at the environment you are in and think about the contribution made to your surroundings by artists and designers. Some may be obvious: there might be a painting on the wall or you could take a look at the front cover of this book. If you are sitting on a chair, consider its design. Is it comfortable? If there is fabric covering the seat, what do you think of the colour and pattern? Look at the clothes you're wearing. Who was responsible for the cut and style? Who designed the fastening on your trousers? Where would you be without that? At home, consider the ergonomic design of your laptop and artwork for the music that you download on it. Think about the packaging of the food that you eat and the shapes of the cutlery that you eat with. Who took the fashion photographs in the magazine that you have just read? Who created the cover design? Who designed the logo? You may have done some research on art schools before reading this chapter – those websites were all designed by someone.

Artists and designers do not just exhibit their work in galleries and exhibitions. They are involved in almost all aspects of our day-to-day living. Artists and designers are concerned with how things look, feel and function. Virtually everything that is manufactured is designed to some extent. Most elements of the media – newspapers, magazines, television, websites, advertising – have considerable input from artists and designers. For every household name that emerges from art school to become rich and famous, there are many thousands of graduates who take up exciting careers that allow them to use their creative talents.

Most students who apply to art and design courses do so because they have a passion for art, and the ability to be creative. Some students say that their intention, after graduating, is to 'become an artist', by which they mean that they would like to use their creative skills in a way that is not manipulated by financial or corporate issues – perhaps they intend to have their own studio, to exhibit their work, and to become respected and admired by those who understand and value what they create. Realistically, however, not everyone has the talent, the focus, the energy or the luck to make a living in this way, and this is of course only one of the options available to those completing a course in art and design.

Working as an artist ...

'Working as an artist, like any other occupation, has its rewards and its drawbacks; it is immensely fulfilling and exciting but also exceptionally hard work. You need to be very self-reliant and resourceful (sometimes even ruthless) to be able to drive a project forward, be it a single work or an exhibition. An artist requires energy, organisational skills, innovation and, of course, insight – as you have to have something to communicate in your work. The best advice I can give is never to stop working – if you don't paint you're a not a painter; if you don't make art you are not an artist. Even when walking down the street I am always looking, always trying to solve pictorial problems or sorting out ideas. Carry sketchbooks, cameras or notebooks; you can't switch off being an artist – you are on duty all the time. An artist's life is never dull or mundane but full of enthusiasm and exciting possibilities. I know few artists who survive entirely by selling their work; they are all uncommonly innovative and part of their professional activities entail teaching, framing, photography, conservation, organising exhibitions, writing, gallery and museum work. An artist's life is an exhilarating but unpredictable journey, full of unexpected twists and stimulating turns but it is not a voyage which should be attempted by the faint-hearted!'

Gerard Hastings
Painter and photographer

'Working as an artist is in not much different from any kind of independent work. Put bluntly, you create a product and hope that people will like it. However, as an artist you need to balance integrity and skill with marketing. People will respect the quality, honesty and individuality of your work. They will appreciate your skills, which will be both your natural abilities combined with hard practice and training. But people can only see your work if you are showing it. Much of your work as an artist is taking your art outside the studio. You can introduce your work to others as a teacher or guest lecturer or artist in residence. You should find opportunities to be with other artists and discuss your work as well as exhibit together. You can also hold solo shows, or solicit projects that can showcase your work. Even if you are not selling, you need to continue to build up a portfolio and stick to your vision. As an artist you are your own boss for better or

worse, but by discipline and integrity, there is no reason why you cannot succeed.'

Ralph Kiggell
Contemporary woodblock artist

'Working as an artist, you experience the ups and downs of life, but I think these mostly happen in your mind. You are constantly learning from your experiences and it is natural that there are many events that you cannot control in your life. Some are good, some are bad, therefore you can be overwhelmingly excited or feel terribly let down. The important thing is to keep yourself steady and carry on with what you are doing. Constant analysis of what happened is always a good opportunity to improve your situation. Art has trends like anything else. You are naturally influenced by those trends when you try to be successful in what you do and you can easily get lost in the current climate. However, you cannot develop your own language fully by following those trends. Your work cannot be imitating other people's ideas.'

Akiko Hirai
Ceramicist

Perhaps a helpful approach when considering career options is to appreciate that the creative skills you possess are key skills. That is to say, your ability to understand and communicate using visual language is as fundamental as being able to understand and use mathematics.

Your talents will always be needed, especially when people are exploring new ideas. Landing on the moon, for example, was a great technological achievement and may not at first seem to have much to do with art and design – but you can be sure that designers were involved every step of the way. Think about it – a footwear designer would have helped to design Neil Armstrong's space boots; perhaps they went on to work for Gucci! Looking at things in this way will help you to keep an open mind.

What do art and design graduates do?

As mentioned earlier, a reasonably high proportion of art and design graduates work on a freelance basis or are self-employed. This can be extremely stimulating and satisfying because you can, to a certain extent, pick and choose the type of work that you wish to undertake. However, it can also be stressful at times because you will need to combine your creative expertise with your skills in business. For some, this is not always a good combination.

Many medium- and large-sized companies employ full-time designers or artists. At the moment, the advertising industry (which employs a large number of art graduates) is suffering a downturn, and work is becoming harder to find within this sector. However, very often when the economy is in a trough, it is advertising and related fields that bounce back first.

Generally, employment rates for art and design graduates are pretty good, with about three-quarters of those looking for work finding it within a few months of graduating – although you need to bear in mind that for some this will mean involvement in short-term projects or contracts. *What Do Graduates Do?* (www.prospects.ac.uk), which is published annually, aims to give a picture of what the graduates from one subject area in one particular year are doing.

Information taken from the publication shows that:

- 2,890 fine art students who graduated in 2007 responded to the survey – 57% were in employment, nearly 20% were undertaking further studies, 13% were working in 'creative' fields.
- 8,950 design graduates responded – 71% were employed; 39% were working in design or creative fields.

Other art and design graduates were working in a variety of jobs, including marketing, sales, public relations, commercial and public-sector management, buying, retailing, catering and general administrative work. In other words, some were using their degrees as a generalist qualification; others were in temporary employment – just like graduates in other subjects. A list of publications that provide information on careers and employment rates is given in Chapter 12. Particularly useful publications are *Design Uncovered* and *Careers in Art and Design*.

Where might your degree lead?

For the purpose of career options, degree courses can be divided into two categories: the fine arts and the applied arts. Examples of the first category include painting, drawing and sculpture, and some photography and textile courses. The second category includes an enormous range of options, such as communications, fashion design, furniture design, art restoration, jewellery design, television and film design, photojournalism and architectural photography. In many of these courses you will be developing skills specifically designed to help you meet employers' needs. If your degree falls into the second category, then you may well find businesses that are looking for someone with your specific qualifications. However, as a fine arts student who, say, used digital manipulation techniques extensively in your work, you can apply to companies that are as interested in your thorough understanding of that particular software program as they are in your ability to consider first principles. This ability to cross over demonstrates the value of key skills and will greatly increase your chances of having a successful working life. Figure 3 will give you some idea of the range of jobs to which specific degree courses might lead you.

Some of the careers that you might consider are:

- accessory design
- animation
- architectural and industrial photography
- architectural glass
- art restoration
- art therapy
- book illustration
- carpet design
- ceramics
- computer games
- costume design
- craft design
- digital imaging
- exhibition design
- fashion design
- fashion photography
- film and video
- glassblowing
- graphic design
- interior decoration
- jewellery
- journalism
- medical illustration
- model making
- museums and galleries

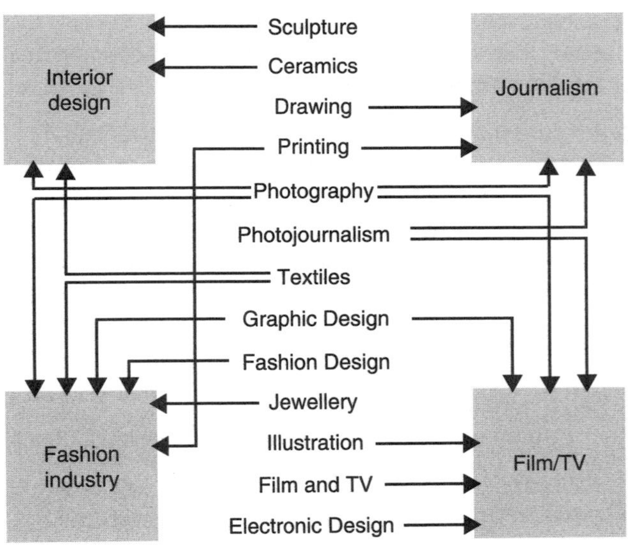

Figure 3 Industry sectors with job opportunities for art and design

- newspaper and magazine design
- packaging design
- printmaking
- public arts
- publishing
- sculpture
- surface pattern design
- tapestry
- teaching
- technical illustration
- textile and fabric design
- theatre design
- video and film production
- web design.

Most universities offer excellent careers advice, but in the case of art and design students, it is important to have thought about possible careers before choosing a degree course. This is why the Foundation course is an important aspect of an art education, because it gives you time to look at degree courses in more detail before committing yourself. Many art and design degree courses are very specialised and will give you a relatively narrow range of options, so you need to be sure that you are choosing a degree course that is going to get you where you want to be.

If you plan to study physics at university (as you are reading this book, you are probably not going to do so!) then you don't need to have a definite idea of what you want to do after graduating, because a physics degree can lead to hundreds of different careers, including those that are not directly related to the subject, such as banking, finance or management. But a degree in costume for performance, for example, offers you fewer options, so you need to be reasonably sure that a career as a ballet or theatre costume designer is what you are aiming for. But don't let this put you off: if you are passionate about research into make-up and know that this is the only thing you want to do, then choose the degree course in cosmetic science, rather than something less focused.

If you are sure that you want a career in a creative field, but at the point of choosing your degree course you are unsure about the exact field, then it might be better to choose something more general, such as fine art or graphic design. In order to get a better idea about possible careers, your research could include:

- work experience
- school or college careers departments
- university websites
- talking to practitioners
- visits to professional bodies (such as the Design Council – see Chapter 12 for contact details).

12 Further information

Applications

Degree courses

UCAS
Rosehill
New Barn Lane
Cheltenham
GL52 3LZ
Tel: 01242 222444
Website: www.ucas.com

Oxford Colleges Admissions Office
University Offices
Wellington Square
Oxford
OX1 2JD
Tel: 01865 288000
Website: www.ox.ac.uk

- *HEAP 2011: University Degree Course Offers*, Brian Heap (Trotman)
- *How to Complete Your UCAS Application: 2011 Entry* (Trotman)
- *University and College Entrance – The Official Guide* (also known as 'the Big Guide') (UCAS)

Funding

- UCAS financial information: www.ucas.com/students/studentfinance
- Student Loans Company: Tel: 0845 300 5090, www.slc.co.uk
- Local authority student support information: www.direct.gov.uk/en and then follow the 'Education and learning' links
- Arts and Humanities Research Council: www.ahrc.ac.uk/FundingOpportunities/
- *Guide to Student Money 2011*, Gwenda Thomas (Trotman)

International students

- British Council: www.britishcouncil.org
- English UK: www.englishuk.com
- UKCISA: www.ukcisa.org

Careers

Careers Uncovered: Design, Karen Holmes (Trotman)
Real Life Guide: Creative Industries, Karen Holmes (Trotman)
Careers in Art and Design, Linda Bell and Noel Chapman (Kogan Page)

Magazines

This list only scrapes the surface of the publications available. The best places to look for art and design magazines are museum and gallery bookshops, which carry wide selections.

- *Ag* (photography)
- *Architectural Journal*
- *Architectural Review*
- *Art Monthly*
- *Art Review*
- *B&W* (photography)
- *Blueprint* (design)
- *British Journal of Photography*
- *Ceramic Review*
- *Ceramics Monthly*
- *Creative Review*
- *Frieze*
- *Modern Painters*
- *Next Level*
- *Photography Monthly*
- *PLUK* (photography listings)
- *Portfolio* (photography)
- *Tate Magazine*

Websites

The web's shifting landscape means that new sites devoted to art and design appear on a daily basis. We have listed some interesting sites below, but you should also do your own searching when you have free time. Searching for 'art magazine online', for example, will give you almost a million starting points.

- A List Apart (web design): www.alistapart.com
- Antidull Magazine: www.antidull.com
- Artkrush Magazine: www.artkrush.com
- Artnet: www.artnet.com
- Art Review: www.artreview.com

- British Arts: www.britisharts.co.uk/artmagazines.htm
- Flash Art: www.flashartonline.com
- Graphic Arts: www.graphicartsonline.com
- Juxtapoz Art & Culture Magazine: www.juxtapoz.com
- NY Arts: www.nyartsmagazine.com
- Saatchi Gallery (links to other resources): www.saatchigallery.co.uk/gallery/links.htm
- Tate Collection: www.tate.org.uk/collection/

Art and design bodies

Arts councils

Arts Council of England
14 Great Peter Street
London
SW1P 3NQ
Website: www.artscouncil.org.uk

Scottish Arts Council
12 Manor Place
Edinburgh
EH3 7DD
Website: www.scottisharts.org.uk

Arts Council of Wales
Bute Place
Cardiff
CF10 5AL
Website: www.artswales.org.uk

Arts Council of Northern Ireland
77 Malone Road
Belfast
BT9 6AQ
Website: www.artscouncil-ni.org

Professional bodies

Association of Photographers
81 Leonard Street
London
EC2A 4QS
Website: www.the-aop.org

British Film Institute
21 Stephen Street
London
W1T 1LN
Website: www.bfi.org.uk

Crafts Council
44a Pentonville Road
London
N1 9BY
Website: www.craftscouncil.org.uk

Design Council
34 Bow Street
London
WC2E 7DL
Website: www.designcouncil.org.uk

Architecture

Architects Registration Board
8 Weymouth Street
London
W1W 5BU
Website: www.arb.org.uk

Royal Institute of British Architects (RIBA)
66 Portland Place
London
W1B 1AD
Website: www.architecture.com

The President's Medals Student Awards
For degree courses in architecture, and examples of students' work see www.presidentsmedals.com.

Artists' websites

- Ralph Kiggell: www.ralphkiggell.com
- Gerard Hastings: www.modernbritishart.net
- Akiko Hirai: www.akikohiraiceramics.com

Appendix

Institution contact details

University of Wales Aberystwyth
Tel: 01970 623111
Email: ug-admissions@aber.ac.uk
Website: www.aber.ac.uk

Amersham and Wycombe College
Buckinghamshire
Tel: 01494 585555
Website: www.amersham.ac.uk

Anglia Ruskin University
Cambridge
Tel: 0845 271 3333
Email: answers@anglia.ac.uk
Website: www.anglia.ac.uk

Arts Institute at Bournemouth
Tel: 01202 533011
Email: general@aib.ac.uk
Website: www.aib.ac.uk

Barking and Dagenham College
Essex
Tel: 01708 770000
Email: admissions@barkingcollege.ac.uk
Website: www.barkingcollege.ac.uk

Barnfield College
Luton
Tel: 01582 569500
Email: enquiries@barnfield.ac.uk
Website: www.barnfield.ac.uk

Barnsley College
Tel: 01226 216216
Email: info@barnsley.ac.uk
Website: www.barnsley.ac.uk

Basingstoke College of Technology
Tel: 01256 354141
Email: information@bcot.ac.uk
Website: www.bcot.ac.uk

Bath Spa University
Tel: 01225 875875
Email: enquiries@bathspa.ac.uk
Website: www.artbathspa.ac.uk

Bedford College
Tel: 01234 291000
Email: info@bedford.ac.uk
Website: www.bedford.ac.uk

University of Bedfordshire
Tel: 01234 400400
Email: admissions@beds.ac.uk
Website: www.beds.ac.uk

University of Birmingham
Tel: 0121 414 3344
Website: www.bham.ac.uk

Birmingham City College
Tel: 08450 501144
Website: www.citycol.ac.uk

Birmingham City University
Tel: 0121 331 5000
Email: choices@bcu.ac.uk
Website: www.bcu.ac.uk, www.biad.bcu.ac.uk

Bishop Burton College
Tel: 01964 553000
Website: www.bishopburton.ac.uk

Bishop Grosseteste University College
Lincoln
Tel: 01522 527347
Email: info@bishopg.ac.uk
Website: www.bishopg.ac.uk

Blackburn College
Tel: 01254 55144
Website: www.blackburn.ac.uk

Blackpool and the Fylde College
Tel: 01253 504442
Website: www.blackpool.ac.uk/amp

University of Bolton
Tel: 01204 903000
Email: enquiries@bolton.ac.uk
Website: www.bolton.ac.uk

Bournemouth University
Tel: 01202 524111
Email: enquiries@bournemouth.ac.uk
Website: www.bournemouth.ac.uk

University of Bradford
Tel: 01274 232323
Email: course-enquiries@bradford.ac.uk
Website: www.brad.ac.uk

Bradford College
Tel: 01274 433333
Website: www.bradfordcollege.ac.uk

University of Brighton
Tel: 01273 600900
Email: enquiries@brighton.ac.uk
Website: www.brighton.ac.uk

Bristol UWE
Tel: 0117 965 6261
Email: admissions@uwe.ac.uk
Website: www.uwe.ac.uk

Bucks New University
Tel: 01494 522141
Email: advice@bucks.ac.uk
Website: www.bucks.ac.uk

Camberwell College of Arts
University of the Arts London
Tel: 020 7514 6302
Email: enquiries@camberwell.arts.ac.uk
Website: www.camberwell.arts.ac.uk

Canterbury Christ Church University
Tel: 01227 767700
Email: admissions@canterbury.ac.uk
Website: www.canterbury.ac.uk

University of Wales Institute (Cardiff)
Tel: 029 2041 6070
Email: admissions@uwic.ac.uk
Website: www.uwic.ac.uk

Carshalton College
Tel: 020 8544 4444
Email: cs@carshalton.ac.uk
Website: www.carshalton.ac.uk

University of Central Lancashire
Tel: 01772 201201
Email: cenquiries@uclan.ac.uk
Website: www.uclan.ac.uk

Central School of Speech and Drama
London
Tel: 020 7722 8183
Email: enquiries@cssd.ac.uk
Website: www.cssd.ac.uk

Central St Martins College of Art and Design
University of the Arts London
Tel: 020 7514 7022
Email: info@csm.arts.ac.uk
Website: www.csm.arts.ac.uk

Chelsea College of Art and Design
University of the Arts London
Tel: 020 7514 7023
Email: enquiries@chelsea.arts.ac.uk
Website: www.chelsea.arts.ac.uk

University of Chester
Tel: 01244 511000
Email: enquiries@chester.ac.uk
Website: www.chester.ac.uk

Chesterfield College
Tel: 01246 500500
Website: www.chesterfield.ac.uk

University of Chichester
Tel: 01243 816000
Email: admissions@chi.ac.uk
Website: www.chiuni.ac.uk

City of Bristol College
Tel: 0117 312 5000
Email: enquiries@cityofbristol.ac.uk
Website: www.cityofbristol.ac.uk

City and Islington College
Tel: 020 7700 9200
Email: courseinfo@candi.ac.uk
Website: www.candi.ac.uk

City College Manchester
Tel: 0800 068 8585
Email: enquiries@themanchestercollege.ac.uk
Website: www.themanchestercollege.ac.uk

City of Sunderland College
Tel: 0191 511 6060
Website: www.citysun.ac.uk

City of Wolverhampton College
Tel: 01902 836000
Email: mail@wolvcoll.ac.uk
Website: www.wolvcoll.ac.uk

Cleveland College of Art and Design
Tel: 01642 288000
Website: www.ccad.ac.uk

Colchester Institute
Tel: 01206 712777
Website: www.colchester.ac.uk

Cornwall College
Tel: 0845 223 2567
Email: enquiries@cornwall.ac.uk
Website: www.cornwall.ac.uk

Coventry University
Tel: 024 7688 7688
Email: studentenquiries@coventry.ac.uk
Website: www.coventry.ac.uk

University for the Creative Arts at Canterbury, Epsom, Farnham, Maidstone and Rochester
Email: admissions@ucreative.ac.uk
Website: www.ucreative.ac.uk

Croydon College
Tel: 020 8686 5700
Email: info@croydon.ac.uk
Website: www.croydon.ac.uk

University of Cumbria
Website: www.cumbria.ac.uk

De Montfort University
Leicester
Tel: 0116 255 1551
Email: enquiry@dmu.ac.uk
Website: www.dmu.ac.uk

University of Derby
Tel: 01332 348846
Email: adtenquiry@derby.ac.uk
Website: www.derby.ac.uk/artanddesign

Doncaster College and University Centre
Tel: 0800 358 7475
Email: infocentre@don.ac.uk
Website: www.don.ac.uk/arts

Dudley College of Technology
Tel: 01384 363000
Email: student.services@dudleycol.ac.uk
Website: www.dudleycol.ac.uk

University of Dundee
Tel: 01382 383000
Email: srs@dundee.ac.uk
Website: www.dundee.ac.uk

University of East Anglia
Norwich
Tel: 01603 456161
Email: admissions@uea.ac.uk
Website: www.uea.ac.uk

University of East London
Tel: 020 8223 3000
Email: study@uel.ac.uk
Website: www.uel.ac.uk

East Surrey College
Tel: 01737 772611
Email: studentservices@esc.ac.uk
Website: www.esc.ac.uk

University of Edinburgh
Tel: 0131 650 1000
Email: communications.office@ed.ac.uk
Website: www.ed.ac.uk

Edinburgh College of Art
Tel: 0131 221 6027
Email: enquiries@eca.ac.uk
Website: www.eca.ac.uk

Edinburgh Napier University
Tel: 0845 260 6040
Email: info@napier.ac.uk
Website: www.napier.ac.uk

Exeter College
Tel: 0845 111 6000
Email: info@exe-coll.ac.uk
Website: www.exe-coll.ac.uk

University College Falmouth
Tel: 01326 211077
Email: admissions@falmouth.ac.uk
Website: www.falmouth.ac.uk

University of Glamorgan
Tel: 01443 480480
Website: www.glam.ac.uk

Glasgow School of Art
Tel: 0141 353 4530
Website: www.gsa.ac.uk

University of Gloucestershire
Tel: 0844 801 0001
Email: admissions@glos.ac.uk
Website: www.glos.ac.uk

Glyndŵr University
Tel: 01978 290666
Email: sid@glyndwr.ac.uk
Website: www.newi.ac.uk

Goldsmiths
University of London
Tel: 020 7919 7766
Email: admissions@gold.ac.uk
Website: www.goldsmiths.ac.uk

University of Greenwich
Tel: 020 8331 8000
Email: courseinfo@greenwich.ac.uk
Website: www.greenwich.ac.uk

University of Hertfordshire
Tel: 01707 284000
Website: www.herts.ac.uk

Herefordshire College of Art and Design
Tel: 01432 273359
Email: enquiries@hca.ac.uk
Website: www.hca.ac.uk

University of Huddersfield
Tel: 01484 422288
Email: admissions@hud.ac.uk
Website: www.hud.ac.uk

Inverness College
UHI Millennium Institute
Tel: 01463 273000
Email: info@inverness.uhi.ac.uk
Website: www.inverness.uhi.ac.uk

University of Kent
Tel: 01227 764000
Email: recruitment@kent.ac.uk
Website: www.kent.ac.uk

Kingston University
Tel: 020 8417 9000
Email: admissions-info@kingston.ac.uk
Website: www.kingston.ac.uk

Kirklees College
Tel: 0500 162100
Email: info@kirkleescollege.ac.uk
Website: www.kirkleescollege.ac.uk

Lancaster Institute for the Contemporary Arts
Lancaster University
Tel: 01524 592702
Email: lica@lancaster.ac.uk
Website: www.lancs.ac.uk/fass/lica

University of Leeds
Tel: 0113 343 1751
Website: www.leeds.ac.uk

Leeds College of Art and Design
Tel: 0113 202 8000
Email: info@leeds-art.ac.uk
Website: www.leeds-art.ac.uk

Leeds Metropolitan University
Tel: 0113 812 3113
Email: courseenquiries@leedsmet.ac.uk
Website: www.leedsmet.ac.uk

Lews Castle College
UHI Millennium Institute
Tel: 01851 770000
Email: enquiries@lews.uhi.ac.uk
Website: www.lews.uhi.ac.uk

University of Lincoln
Tel: 01522 882000
Email: aadmarketing@lincoln.ac.uk
Website: www.lincoln.ac.uk/aad

Liverpool Hope University
Tel: 0151 291 3295
Email: admission@hope.ac.uk
Website: www.hope.ac.uk

Liverpool John Moores University
Tel: 0151 231 1212
Website: www.livjm.ac.uk

London College of Communication
University of the Arts London
Tel: 020 7514 6569
Email: info@lcc.arts.ac.uk
Website: www.lcc.arts.ac.uk

London College of Fashion
University of the Arts London
Tel: 020 7514 7344
Email: enquiries@fashion.arts.ac.uk
Website: www.fashion.arts.ac.uk

London Metropolitan University
Tel: 020 7133 4200
Email: admissions@londonmet.ac.uk
Website: www.londonmet.ac.uk

University College London
Tel: 020 7679 2000
Website: www.ucl.ac.uk

Loughborough University
Tel: 01509 263171
Website: www.lboro.ac.uk

Lowestoft College
Tel: 01502 500031
Website: www.lowestoft.ac.uk

Manchester Metropolitan University
Tel: 0161 247 2000
Email: enquiries@mmu.ac.uk
Website: www.mmu.ac.uk

Middlesex University
Tel: 020 8411 5555
Email: enquiries@mdx.ac.uk
Website: www.mdx.ac.uk

Moray College
UHI Millennium Institute
Tel: 01343 576000
Email: mc.registry@moray.uhi.ac.uk
Website: www.moray.ac.uk

Newcastle University
Tel: 0191 222 6000
Website: www.ncl.ac.uk

Newcastle College
Tel: 0191 200 4000
Email: enquiries@ncl-coll.ac.uk
Website: www.ncl-coll.ac.uk

New College Nottingham
Tel: 0115 910 0100
Email: enquiries@ncn.ac.uk
Website: www.ncn.ac.uk

University of Wales Newport
Tel: 01633 430088
Email: uic@newport.ac.uk
Website: www.newport.ac.uk

University of Northampton
Tel: 0800 358 2232
Email: study@northampton.ac.uk
Website: www.northampton.ac.uk

Northbrook College Sussex
Tel: 0845 155 6060
Email: enquiries@nbcol.ac.uk
Website: www.northbrook.ac.uk

Northumbria University
Tel: 0871 432 6562
Email: er.admissions@northumbria.ac.uk
Website: www.northumbria.ac.uk

Norwich School of Art and Design
Tel: 01603 610561
Email: info@nsad.ac.uk
Website: www.nsad.ac.uk

Nottingham Trent University
Tel: 0115 941 8418
Email: ntsad@ntu.ac.uk
Website: www.ntu.ac.uk

Orkney College
UHI Millennium Institute
Tel: 01856 569000
Email: orkney.college@uhi.ac.uk
Website: www.orkney.uhi.ac.uk

The Ruskin School of Drawing and Fine Art
University of Oxford
Tel: 01865 276940
Website: www.ruskin-sch.ox.ac.uk

Oxford and Cherwell Valley College
Tel: 01865 550550
Email: enquiries@ocvc.ac.uk
Website: www.ocvc.ac.uk

Oxford Brookes University
Tel: 01865 484848
Email: query@brookes.ac.uk
Website: www.brookes.ac.uk

Perth College
UHI Millennium Institute
Tel: 0845 270 1177
Email: pc.admissions@perth.uhi.ac.uk
Website: www.perth.ac.uk

University of Plymouth
Tel: 01752 585858
Email: arts.admissions@plymouth.ac.uk
Website: www.plymouth.ac.uk/arts

Plymouth College of Art and Design
Tel: 01752 203434
Email: enquiries@plymouthart.ac.uk
Website: www.plymouthart.ac.uk

University of Portsmouth
Tel: 023 9284 8484
Email: info.centre@port.ac.uk
Website: www.port.ac.uk

University of Reading
Tel: 0118 378 7383
Email: fineart@reading.ac.uk
Website: www.rdg.ac.uk/fineart

Richmond, the American International University in London
Tel: 020 8332 9000
Email: enroll@richmond.ac.uk
Website: www.richmond.ac.uk

Robert Gordon University
Tel: 01224 646346
Email: admissions@rgu.ac.uk
Website: www.rgu.ac.uk/grays

Roehampton University
Tel: 020 8392 3232
Email: enquiries@roehampton.ac.uk
Website: www.roehampton.ac.uk

SAE Institute
London
Tel: 020 7923 9159
Email: saelondon@sae.edu
Website: www.saeuk.com

St Martin's College
See University of Cumbria
Website: www.cumbria.ac.uk

University of Salford
Tel: 0161 295 5000
Email: course-enquiries@salford.ac.uk
Website: www.salford.ac.uk

Sheffield Hallam University
Tel: 0114 225 5555
Email: enquiries@shu.ac.uk
Website: www.shu.ac.uk

Shrewsbury College of Arts and Technology
Tel: 01743 342333
Email: prospects@shrewsbury.ac.uk
Website: www.shrewsbury.ac.uk

Coleg Sir Gâr
Carmarthenshire College
Tel: 01554 748000
Email: admissions@colegsirgar.ac.uk
Website: www.colegsirgar.ac.uk

Solihull College
Tel: 0121 678 7000
Email: enquiries@solihull.ac.uk
Website: www.solihull.ac.uk

Somerset College of Arts and Technology
Tel: 01823 366366
Email: enquiries@somerset.ac.uk
Website: www.somerset.ac.uk

South Essex College
Southend
Tel: 01702 220400
Email: learning@southessex.ac.uk
Website: www.southessex.ac.uk

University of Southampton
Tel: 023 8059 5000
Email: admissns@soton.ac.uk
Website: www.soton.ac.uk

Southampton Solent University
Tel: 023 8031 9000
Email: ask@solent.ac.uk
Website: www.solent.ac.uk

Southport College
Tel: 01704 500606
Website: www.southport.ac.uk

Staffordshire University and Staffordshire University Regional Federation
Tel: 01782 294000
Email: admissions@staffs.ac.uk
Website: www.staffs.ac.uk

Stockport College
Tel: 0161 958 3100
Email: admissions@stockport.ac.uk
Website: www.stockport.ac.uk

Suffolk New College
Tel: 01473 255885
Email: info@suffolk.ac.uk
Website: www.suffolk.ac.uk

University of Sunderland
Tel: 0191 515 3000
Email: student.helpline@sunderland.ac.uk
Website: www.sunderland.ac.uk

Swansea Metropolitan University
Tel: 01792 481000
Email: enquiry@smu.ac.uk
Website: www.smu.ac.uk

Swindon College
Tel: 01793 491591
Email: studentservices@swindon-college.ac.uk
Website: www.swindon-college.ac.uk

University of Teesside
Tel: 01642 342067
Email: arts@tees.ac.uk
Website: www.tees.ac.uk

Thames Valley University
Tel: 0800 036 8888
Website: www.tvu.ac.uk

Trinity College
Carmarthen
Tel: 01267 676767
Website: www.trinity-cm.ac.uk

University of Ulster
Tel: 08700 400700
Website: www.ulster.ac.uk

University of the West of Scotland
Paisley Campus
Tel: 0141 848 3000
Email: info@uws.ac.uk
Website: www.uws.ac.uk

West Suffolk College
Tel: 01284 701301
Email: info@wsc.ac.uk
Website: www.westsuffolk-ac.co.uk

West Thames College
London
Tel: 020 8326 2000
Email: info@west-thames.ac.uk
Website: www.west-thames.ac.uk

University of Westminster
Tel: 020 7911 5000
Email: course-enquiries@westminster.ac.uk
Website: www.westminster.ac.uk

Westminster Kingsway College
Tel: 0870 060 9800
Email: courseinfo@westking.ac.uk
Website: www.westking.ac.uk

Weston College
Tel: 01934 411411
Email: enquiries@weston.ac.uk
Website: www.weston.ac.uk

Weymouth College
Tel: 01305 761100
Email: igs@weymouth.ac.uk
Website: www.weymouth.ac.uk

Wigan and Leigh College
Tel: 01942 761600
Website: www.wigan-leigh.ac.uk

Wiltshire College
Tel: 01225 350035
Email: info@wiltshire.ac.uk
Website: www.wiltshire.ac.uk

Wimbledon College of Art
University of the Arts London
Tel: 020 7514 9687
Email: info@wimbledon.arts.ac.uk
Website: www.wimbledon.arts.ac.uk

Wirral Metropolitan College
Tel: 0151 551 7777
Website: www.wmc.ac.uk

University of Wolverhampton
Tel: 01902 321000
Email: enquiries@wlv.ac.uk
Website: www.wlv.ac.uk

University of Worcester
Tel: 01905 855000
Email: study@worc.ac.uk
Website: www.worc.ac.uk

Worcester College of Technology
Tel: 01905 725555
Email: college@wortech.ac.uk
Website: www.wortech.ac.uk

Writtle College
Tel: 01245 424200
Email: info@writtle.ac.uk
Website: www.writtle.ac.uk

University Centre Yeovil
Tel: 01935 845454
Email: ucy@yeovil.ac.uk
Website: www.ucy.ac.uk

York College
Tel: 01904 770400
Email: enrolment@yorkcollege.ac.uk
Website: www.yorkcollege.ac.uk

York St John University
Tel: 01904 624624
Email: admissions@yorksj.ac.uk
Website: www.yorksj.ac.uk

Yorkshire Coast College
Tel: 01723 372 105
Email: enquiries@ycoastco.ac.uk
Website: www.yorkshirecoastcollege.ac.uk

Non-UCAS institutions

Aberdeen College
Tel: 01224 612000
Email: enquiry@abcol.ac.uk
Website: www.abcol.ac.uk

Abingdon and Witney College
Tel: 01235 555585
Email: enquiry@abingdon-witney.ac.uk
Website: www.abingdon-witney.ac.uk

Accrington and Rossendale College
Tel: 01254 354354
Email: info@accross.ac.uk
Website: www.accross.ac.uk

Adam Smith College
Tel: 0800 413280
Email: enquiries@adamsmith.ac.uk
Website: www.adamsmith.ac.uk

Alton College
Hampshire
Tel: 01420 592200
Email: enquiries@altoncollege.ac.uk
Website: www.altoncollege.ac.uk

Angus College
Tel: 01241 432600
Website: www.angus.ac.uk

Anniesland College
Glasgow
Tel: 0141 357 3969
Email: reception@anniesland.ac.uk
Website: www.anniesland.ac.uk

Ayr College
Tel: 01292 265184
Email: enquiries@ayrcoll.ac.uk
Website: www.ayrcoll.ac.uk

Banff and Buchan College
Tel: 01346 586100
Email: info@banff-buchan.ac.uk
Website: www.banff-buchan.ac.uk

Barnet College
Tel: 020 8266 4000
Website: www.barnet.ac.uk

Barrow in Furness Sixth Form College
Tel: 01229 825017
Email: principal@barrow6fc.ac.uk
Website: www.barrow6fc.ac.uk

Barry College
Tel: 01446 725000
Website: www.barry.ac.uk

Belfast Metropolitan College
Tel: 028 9026 5265
Email: Central_Admissions@belfastmet.ac.uk
Website: www.belfastmet.ac.uk

Bexley College
Tel: 01332 404000
Website: www.bexley.ac.uk

Blake College
London
Tel: 020 7636 0658
Email: study@blake.ac.uk
Website: www.blake.ac.uk

Borders College
Tel: 0870 050 5152
Email: enquiries@borderscollege.ac.uk
Website: www.borderscollege.ac.uk

Bournemouth and Poole College
Tel: 01202 205205
Email: enquiries@thecollege.co.uk
Website: www.thecollege.co.uk

Bracknell and Wokingham College
Tel: 01344 778536
Email: study@bracknell.ac.uk
Website: www.bracknell.ac.uk

Braintree College
Tel: 01376 321711
Email: enquiries@braintree.ac.uk
Website: www.braintree.ac.uk

Bridgend College
Tel: 01656 302302
Email: enquiries@bridgend.ac.uk
Website: www.bridgend.ac.uk

Bristol Old Vic Theatre School
Tel: 0117 973 3535
Email: enquiries@oldvic.ac.uk
Website: www.oldvic.ac.uk

Brooklands College
Weybridge
Tel: 01932 797797
Email: info@brooklands.ac.uk
Website: www.brooklands.ac.uk

Burnley College
Tel: 01282 733373
Email: student.services@burnley.ac.uk
Website: www.burnley.ac.uk

Bury College
Tel: 0161 280 8280
Email: information@burycollege.ac.uk
Website: www.burycollege.ac.uk

Calderdale College
Halifax
Tel: 01422 357357
Email: info@calderdale.ac.uk
Website: www.calderdale.ac.uk

Cambridge Regional College
Tel: 01223 418200
Email: enquiry@camre.ac.uk
Website: www.camre.ac.uk

Cambridge School of Visual and Performing Arts
Tel: 01223 314431
Email: enquiries@csvpa.com
Website: www.csvpa.com

Cannock Chase Technical College
Tel: 01543 462200
Email: enquiries@cannock.ac.uk
Website: www.cannock.ac.uk

Cardonald College Glasgow
Tel: 0141 272 3333
Email: enquiries@cardonald.ac.uk
Website: www.cardonald.ac.uk

Carmel College
Tel: 01744 452200
Email: info@carmel.ac.uk
Website: www.carmel.ac.uk

Carnegie College
Tel: 01383 845000
Email: info@carnegiecollege.ac.uk
Website: www.carnegiecollege.ac.uk

Cavendish College
London
Tel: 020 7580 4074
Email: learn@cavendish.ac.uk
Website: www.cavendish.ac.uk

Central College of Commerce
Glasgow
Tel: 0141 552 3941
Website: www.centralcollege.ac.uk

Christie's Education
London
Tel: 020 7665 4350
Email: education@christies.com
Website: www.christies.com/education

City and Guilds of London Art School
Tel: 020 7735 2306
Email: info@cityandguildsartschool.ac.uk
Website: www.cityandguildsartschool.ac.uk

City College Brighton and Hove
Tel: 01273 667788
Email: info@ccb.ac.uk
Website: www.ccb.ac.uk

City Literary Institute
Tel: 020 7831 7831
Email: infoline@citylit.ac.uk
Website: www.citylit.ac.uk

City of Bath College
Tel: 01225 312191
Email: enquiries@citybathcoll.ac.uk
Website: www.citybathcoll.ac.uk

Clydebank College
Tel: 0141 951 7400
Email: info@clydebank.ac.uk
Website: www.clydebank.ac.uk

Cornwall College
Tel: 0845 223 2567
Email: enquiries@cornwall.ac.uk
Website: www.cornwall.ac.uk

Craven College
Skipton
Tel: 01756 791411
Email: enquiries@craven-college.ac.uk
Website: www.craven-college.ac.uk

Deeside College
Flintshire
Tel: 01244 831531
Website: www.deeside.ac.uk

Derby College
Tel: 01332 520200
Email: enquiries@derby-college.ac.uk
Website: www.derby-college.ac.uk

Dumfries and Galloway College
Tel: 01387 734000
Email: info@dumgal.ac.uk
Website: www.dumgal.ac.uk

Dundee College
Tel: 01382 834800
Email: enquiry@dundeecollege.ac.uk
Website: www.dundeecollege.ac.uk

Dunstable College
Tel: 0845 355 2525
Email: enquiries@centralbeds.ac.uk
Website: www.dunstable.ac.uk

Ealing, Hammersmith and West London College
Tel: 0800 034 6474
Email: cic@wlc.ac.uk
Website: www.wlc.ac.uk

East Berkshire College
Tel: 0845 373 2500
Email: info@eastberks.ac.uk
Website: www.eastberks.ac.uk

East Riding College
Tel: 0845 120 0037
Website: www.eastridingcollege.ac.uk

East Tyrone College of Further and Higher Education
Tel: 028 8676 2620
Email: info@etcfhe.ac.uk
Website: www.etcfhe.ac.uk

Easton College
Tel: 01603 731200
Email: info@easton-college.ac.uk
Website: www.easton-college.ac.uk

Edinburgh's Telford College
Tel: 0131 559 4000
Email: mail@ed-coll.ac.uk
Website: www.ed-coll.ac.uk

Elmwood College
Fife
Tel: 01334 470047
Website: www.elmwood.ac.uk

Enfield College
Tel: 020 8443 3434
Email: courseinformation@enfield.ac.uk
Website: www.conel.ac.uk

Filton College
Tel: 0117 931 2121
Email: info@filton.ac.uk
Website: www.filton.ac.uk

Forth Valley College
Tel: 01786 406080
Website: www.forthvalley.ac.uk

Gateshead College
Tel: 0191 490 0300
Website: www.gateshead.ac.uk

Glasgow Metropolitan College
Tel: 0141 566 6222
Email: enquiries@glasgowmet.ac.uk
Website: www.glasgowmet.ac.uk

Grantham College
Tel: 01476 400200
Website: www.grantham.ac.uk

Greenwich Community College
Tel: 020 8488 4800
Email: info@gcc.ac.uk
Website: www.gcc.ac.uk

Coleg Gwent
Tel: 01495 333333
Email: info@coleggwent.ac.uk
Website: www.coleggwent.ac.uk

Harrow College
Tel: 020 8909 6000
Email: enquiries@harrow.ac.uk
Website: www.harrow.ac.uk

Heatherley's School of Fine Art
London
Tel: 020 7351 4190
Email: info@heatherleys.org
Website: www.heatherleys.org

Henley College
Tel: 01491 579988
Email: info@henleycol.ac.uk
Website: www.henleycol.ac.uk

Hereward College
Coventry
Tel: 024 7646 1231
Email: enquiries@hereward.ac.uk
Website: www.hereward.ac.uk

Hugh Baird College
Bootle
Tel: 0151 353 4444
Email: enquiries@hughbaird.ac.uk
Website: www.hughbaird.ac.uk

Huntingdonshire Regional College
Tel: 01480 379100
Email: college@huntingdon.ac.uk
Website: www.huntingdon.ac.uk

Isle of Man College
Tel: 01624 648200
Website: www.iomcollege.ac.im

James Watt College
Tel: 0800 587 2277
Email: enquiries@jameswatt.ac.uk
Website: www.jameswatt.ac.uk

Jewel and Esk College
Edinburgh
Tel: 0131 344 7100
Website: www.jevc.ac.uk

Keighley College
Tel: 01535 685000
Website: www.keighley.ac.uk

Kendal College
Tel: 01539 814700
Email: enquiries@kendal.ac.uk
Website: www.kendal.ac.uk

Kensington and Chelsea College
Tel: 020 7573 3600
Email: enquiries@kcc.ac.uk
Website: www.kcc.ac.uk

Kilmarnock College
Tel: 01563 523501
Email: enquiries@kilmarnock.ac.uk
Website: www.kilmarnock.ac.uk

Kingston College
Tel: 020 8546 2151
Email: info@kingston-college.ac.uk
Website: www.kingston-college.ac.uk

Knowsley Community College
Merseyside
Tel: 0845 155 1055
Email: info@knowsleycollege.ac.uk
Website: www.knowsleycollege.ac.uk

Langside College
Glasgow
Tel: 0141 272 3600
Email: enquireuk@langside.ac.uk
Website: www.langside.ac.uk

Leeds City College
Technology Campus
Tel: 0113 297 6464
Email: info@lct.ac.uk
Website: www.lct.ac.uk

Leek College of Further Education and School of Art
Tel: 01538 398866
Email: admissions@leek.ac.uk
Website: www.leek.ac.uk

Leith School of Art
Edinburgh
Tel: 0131 554 5761
Website: www.leithschoolofart.co.uk

Lincoln College
Tel: 01522 876000
Email: enquiries@lincolncollege.ac.uk
Website: www.lincolncollege.ac.uk

Luton Sixth Form College
Tel: 01582 412005
Email: info@lutonsfc.ac.uk
Website: www.lutonsfc.ac.uk

Macclesfield College
Tel: 01625 410000
Email: college@macclesfield.ac.uk
Website: www.macclesfield.ac.uk

Coleg Meirion-Dwyfor
Dolgellau
Tel: 01758 701385
Email: coleg@meirion-dwyfor.ac.uk
Website: www.meirion-dwyfor.ac.uk

Milton Keynes College
Tel: 01908 684444
Website: www.mkcollege.ac.uk

Coleg Morgannwg
Pontypridd
Tel: 01443 662800
Email: college@pontypridd.ac.uk
Website: www.pontypridd.ac.uk

Morley College
London
Tel: 020 7450 9226
Email: enquiries@morleycollege.ac.uk
Website: www.morleycollege.ac.uk

Motherwell College
Tel: 01698 232452
Email: information@motherwell.ac.uk
Website: www.motherwell.ac.uk

Nelson and Colne College
Tel: 01282 440200
Email: reception@nelson.ac.uk
Website: www.nelson.ac.uk

Newbury College
Tel: 01635 845000
Email: info@newbury-college.ac.uk
Website: www.newbury-college.ac.uk

North Devon College
Tel: 01271 345291
Email: postbox@ndevon.ac.uk
Website: www.ndevon.ac.uk

College of North East London
Tel: 020 8802 3111
Website: www.conel.ac.uk

North Glasgow College
Tel: 0141 558 9001
Website: www.north-gla.ac.uk

North Hertfordshire College
Tel: 01462 424242
Email: enquiries@nhc.ac.uk
Website: www.nhc.ac.uk

North Lindsey College
Tel: 01724 281111
Email: info@northlindsey.ac.uk
Website: www.northlindsey.ac.uk

College of North West London
Tel: 020 8208 5000
Email: cic@cnwl.ac.uk
Website: www.cnwl.ac.uk

North West Regional College
Tel: 028 7127 6000 (Derry/Londonderry);
028 7127 8700 (Limavady);
028 7138 2317 (Strabane)
Website: www.nwrc.ac.uk

Oaklands College
Welwyn Garden City
Tel: 01727 737000
Email: advice.centre@oaklands.ac.uk
Website: www.oaklands.ac.uk

Coleg Powys
Tel: 0845 408 6400 (Brecon);
0845 408 6300 (Llandrindod);
0845 408 6200 (Newtown);
01639 849234 (Ystradgynlais)
Email: enquiries@coleg-powys.ac.uk
Website: www.coleg-powys.ac.uk

Priestley College
Warrington
Tel: 01925 633591
Email: enquiries@priestley.ac.uk
Website: www.priestley.ac.uk

Prince's School of Traditional Arts
London
Tel: 020 7613 8500
Email: enquiry@psta.org.uk
Website: www.psta.org.uk

Queen Elizabeth Sixth Form College
Darlington
Tel: 01325 461315
Email: enquiry@qeliz.ac.uk
Website: www.qeliz.ac.uk

Reid Kerr College
Paisley
Tel: 0141 581 2222
Email: sservices@reidkerr.ac.uk
Website: www.reidkerr.ac.uk

Richmond Adult Community College
Twickenham
Tel: 020 8891 5907
Email: info@racc.ac.uk
Website: www.racc.ac.uk

Richmond upon Thames College
Tel: 020 8607 8000
Email: courses@rutc.ac.uk
Website: www.rutc.ac.uk

Royal Academy Schools
London
Tel: 020 7300 5857
Email: schools@royalacademy.org.uk
Website: www.royalacademy.org.uk/raschools

Royal College of Art
London
Tel: 020 7590 4444
Email: admissions@rca.ac.uk
Website: www.rca.ac.uk

Runshaw College
Preston
Tel: 01772 622677
Website: www.runshaw.ac.uk

Selby College
Tel: 01757 211000
Website: www.selby.ac.uk

Sotheby's Institute of Art
London
Tel: 020 7462 3232
Email: info@sothebysinstitute.com
Website: www.sothebysinstitute.com

South East Derbyshire College
Tel: 0115 849 2000
Email: admissions@sedc.ac.uk
Website: www.sedc.ac.uk

South Eastern Regional College
Tel: 0845 600 7555
Email: info@serc.ac.uk
Website: www.serc.ac.uk

South Kent College
Tel: 0845 207 8220
Website: www.southkent.ac.uk

South Thames College
London
Tel: 020 8918 7777
Email: studentservices@south-thames.ac.uk
Website: www.south-thames.ac.uk

Southern Regional College
Email: info@src.ac.uk
Website: www.src.ac.uk

Southgate College
Tel: 020 8982 5050
Email: admiss@southgate.ac.uk
Website: www.southgate.ac.uk

Stevenson College
Edinburgh
Tel: 0131 535 4600
Email: info@stevenson.ac.uk
Website: www.stevenson.ac.uk

Stourbridge College
Tel: 01384 344344
Email: info@stourbridge.ac.uk
Website: www.stourbridge.ac.uk

Strode College
Street
Tel: 01458 844400
Website: www.strode-college.ac.uk

Stroud College
Gloucestershire
Tel: 01453 763424
Email: enquire@stroud.ac.uk
Website: www.stroud.ac.uk

Sussex Coast College Hastings
Tel: 01424 442222
Email: studentadvisers@sussexcoast.ac.uk
Website: www.sussexcoast.ac.uk

Sussex Downs College
Email: info@sussexdowns.ac.uk
Website: www.sussexdowns.ac.uk

Telford College of Arts and Technology
Tel: 01952 642237
Website: www.tcat.ac.uk

Thanet College
Tel: 01843 605040
Website: www.thanet.ac.uk

Tower Hamlets College
Tel: 020 7510 7777
Website: www.tower.ac.uk

Tresham Institute of Further and Higher Education
Tel: 0845 658 8990
Email: info@tresham.ac.uk
Website: www.tresham.ac.uk

Truro College
Tel: 01872 267000
Website: www.trurocollege.ac.uk

Walford and North Shropshire College
Tel: 01691 688000
Email: enquiries@wnsc.ac.uk
Website: www.wnsc.ac.uk

Waltham Forest College
Tel: 020 8501 8501
Email: info@waltham.ac.uk
Website: www.waltham.ac.uk

Warwickshire College
Tel: 0845 217 7414
Email: enquiries@warkscol.ac.uk
Website: www.warkscol.ac.uk

College of West Anglia
Wisbech
Tel: 01945 581024
Email: enquiries@col-westanglia.ac.uk
Website: www.col-westanglia.ac.uk

West Cheshire College
Tel: 01244 677677
Email: info@west-cheshire.ac.uk
Website: www.west-cheshire.ac.uk

West Dean College
Tel: 01243 811301
Email: enquiries@westdean.org.uk
Website: www.westdean.org.uk

West Kent College
Tel: 01732 358101
Email: enquiries@wkc.ac.uk
Website: www.wkc.ac.uk

West Lothian College
Tel: 01506 418181
Email: enquiries@west-lothian.ac.uk
Website: www.west-lothian.ac.uk

West Nottinghamshire College
Tel: 01623 627191
Website: www.westnotts.ac.uk

City of Westminster College
Tel: 020 7723 8826
Email: customer.services@cwc.ac.uk
Website: www.cwc.ac.uk

Winstanley College
Wigan
Tel: 01695 633244
Website: www.winstanley.ac.uk

Yale College of Wrexham
Tel: 01978 311794
Email: admissions@yale-wrexham.ac.uk
Website: www.yale-wrexham.co.uk